Write
the Story
of Your Life

Write the Story of Your Life

Ruth Kanin

Hawthorn/Dutton · New York

For information contact:
Elsevier-Dutton Publishing Co., Inc.,
2 Park Avenue, New York, N.Y. 10016

Library of Congress Cataloging in Publication Data
Kanin, Ruth.
Write the story of your life.
1. Autobiography.   I. Title.
CT25.K28   808'.06692021   80–20653
ISBN: 0-8015-3871-8 (cloth)
ISBN: 0-8015-8930-4 (paper)

Published simultaneously in Canada by Clarke, Irwin & Company Limited,
Toronto and Vancouver

Designed by Barbara Cohen

10 9 8 7 6 5 4 3 2 1

First Edition

For my parents

Sadie Kanin
(1890–1979)

David Kanin
(1885–1948)

Contents

4. ADULTHOOD   61

*What is important?   Missing or minimized parts
Selecting your own stages   Categories of adulthood*

5. PRUNING YOUR ROOTS   70

*Harvesting historical data   Getting your material
organized   Special problems*

6. THE SUBLIMINAL SELF   81

*Psychological theories and tools for self-understanding
Defense mechanisms (repression, denial, reaction
formation, projection, rationalization, withdrawal,
fixation, and martyrdom)   The four functions of
C. G. Jung   Transactional analysis: Eric Berne
Self-actualization: Maslow   Behavior modification
Assertiveness training   Relaxation   Concentration
Self-hypnosis   Meditation   Dreams   Sample tape for
self-hypnosis*

7. DIARIES, JOURNALS, AND OTHER RAW
MATERIAL   99

*Reasons for writing diaries and their value   Other raw
material   Finding your own system and way of starting
Techniques   Rereading old diaries   Privacy and
paranoia   Dialogues   Unsent letters   Your audience*

*Narration   Transitions   The novel   The short story
The dramatized diary*

*Lengths and layouts: preparing the manuscript
Revising and polishing   Story checklist (overview, the
story, the writing, the characters, structure, clarity,
unity, style)   Marketing and the publishing scene*

Foreword

We all applaud a winner—in particular the winner not by chance but by reason of ambition, setting an objective, planning, working hard, and finally achieving the goal. Ruth Kanin is such a winner.

When the goal also achieves results that help not only the winner but others as well, it's a double win. Ruth Kanin is such a double winner.

Dr. Kanin's book, which you are about to read, was originally the culmination of a learning process she undertook with International College in pursuit of a higher degree. As a dissertation, it was to demonstrate all she knew and had additionally learned about autobiography as a literary and therapeutic form through history, and how it can serve not only the famous and infamous, but all of us as a means of self-therapy, as an outlet for our own sense of history, family, and tradition, and as a way of breaking into the demanding task of writing for others. Her research led Dr. Kanin into how to best accomplish this, and how to get the results into print, even perhaps profitably. This book is the refined, nonacademic result of her tutorial with International College.

I believe that the many would-be writers, and even those who already have successfully broken the block, will find what Dr. Kanin has to say of great value and help. Not the least help can come from the appreciation that she herself broke through, and that success in writing has more to do with will and hard work than it does with luck. Like any other craft, it is demanding, but the process can be pleasurable and the rewards of achievement—whether or not you are published—great. The process of creation is one that is natural to all of us and for which we naturally seek outlets. The written word is one of humankind's most enduring—and certainly its most important—form of creation. To share in this tradition, whether we create for many readers or a few, can be one of life's richest pleasures. If royalties flow from the result, the pleasure is double. But the real reward, you will find, is in the process of personal growth that the autobiographical experience can bring you.

PAUL O. PROEHL
President, International College

Acknowledgments

To the many students, clients, friends, and relatives who participated in the workshops and helped to shape the text and exercises, especially Women Writers West for their warm and cooperative responses. Special thanks to Elaine and Gar Greene, Doris Siegel, and Gerry and Nat Gladstone.

To my friends who encouraged me and helped in many wonderful ways, especially Olga Druce, Ruth Gilbert, Nancy Gross, Ruth Hill, Dorothy and Murray Hirsch, Cylvia Margulies, Flora Mock, Meri von Sternberg, and Isabelle Ziegler.

To the good people at International College, including Charlotte Metz, and especially Cornelia Leavitt and Paul Proehl.

To my agent and friend, the late Ruth Hagy Brod, who believed in me.

To my editor, Constance Schrader, whose warmth and patience helped me expand my belief in myself.

To my brothers, Garson and Michael, who bugged me to write since my first letter home from camp.

To my daughters, Cass and Dena, my extraspecial thanks for their emotional support, friendship, and love.

Introduction

At the age of nineteen I dropped out of college to see the world. After thirty-one years I returned. I had seen the world. I didn't like it.

Homemaking and motherhood had given me a plus I wouldn't trade for anything, but the act of juggling the endless skills required for those jobs produced a minus: part of my brain became rusty. I had trouble concentrating and making decisions, especially about my professional goal.

I had lost a husband along the way (to a college-aged girl, when our children were very small). My daughters were now grown and about to go off and see the world for themselves.

Reentry into college entailed problems: poor grades in my early college years, spinal injuries from an auto accident, low energy, fear of studying, terror of taking written tests, inadequate funds, and low self-esteem.

Not much to build on, but alternatives were bleak.

Two years later I took my bachelor's degree *summa cum laude*, at the top of my class.

A reporter thought this newsworthy and came to write an article about me.

"Me? Who wants to hear about *my* life?" (I hadn't yet mastered the self-esteem part.)

"Hasn't anyone told you that you're doing something courageous?"

"No. Everyone thinks I've gone mad. And I thought I was just struggling."

She looked at me quizzically. "Don't you realize that there

must be thousands of women out there who would like to do better with their lives but don't try because they think they're too old, sick, poor, or stupid? You can be an inspiration to them!"

The article appeared, followed by hundreds of letters and phone calls clamoring for my "secrets" of how-to.

A literary agent called. She wanted to represent me for the story of my life. I was an inspiration, she said.

I still couldn't see the point of writing my story until a few years later.

My mother's health began to fail. Depression replaced her usual good spirits. She became obsessed with the past, brooding over the mistakes, lost opportunities, and lack of fulfillment. To help restore her sense of self-worth, I began to tape an oral history of her life and times.

Something happened to both of us as a result. I realized there was much about her life I never knew. She hadn't bothered to tell me, thinking it unimportant, and I hadn't bothered to ask, assuming it was uninteresting. As I learned about her early life, my understanding of her and her generation grew—how America shaped them and how they shaped America.

As she piled up her positive experiences, she gained a sense of having lived a worthwhile life, reassured that she had done her best. Her worst fears—of having failed as a mother—were calmed.

My own daughters knew little of my early life. If I wanted them to understand me fully, I had better write my story, but with a new respect for my own experiences and a better attitude. I began to put together my personal history for our family record and for self-examination. This project did more for me than a potpourri of therapies.

Books and guidance on the craft of autobiography were scarce, so I developed a system through book research, interviews, and workshops with students and clients. I found there were common problems people faced in writing their stories, and common solutions. We all agreed a book was needed with the collected information, and I decided to write this one first. My autobiography would have to wait.

Consider this book a traveling companion on your journey backward into time and forward into an expanded view of yourself and your times. You'll be given tools and techniques to fortify you against any fears of dredging up memories, and you'll learn ways to draw on your memory bank. You'll discover the numberless ways to tell your story. The miseries and mysteries of the act of writing will be penetrated.

You can work alone with this book, but if you have trouble with self-motivation, get together with one or more others. If you meet regularly, sharing, you'll be surprised how this will develop discipline and productivity.

Autobiography is among the most popular book forms today. In the past, only stories of famous people were thought worth reading. Now, anyone's story that is entertaining, inspirational, enlightening, and well written is being enjoyed. At this time, some of these are: a woman's story of her mastectomy (being made into a film); a man's sea voyage in a small craft; a seventy-two-year-old woman's family history told in her authentic "unschooled" European accent; and a real-estate broker's anecdotes about selling houses.

Most students who undertook this project experienced relief from puzzles and ghosts haunting their past. Their goals were more sharply defined. When they were able to accept *all* of life's experiences, their rewards were major life changes.

Writing the story of your life can be your most complete and satisfying experience, whether your goal is to be an author, a family historian, or the greatest authority on the subject of you.

Write
the Story
of Your Life

1

Why Write Your Story?

> *The next thing most like living one's life over again seems to be a recollection of that life, and to make that recollection as durable as possible by putting it down in writing.*
>
> —BENJAMIN FRANKLIN

You've bought or borrowed this book, so you have been thinking about writing your story. Maybe you've started but gotten discouraged or bogged down. Problems popped up: How can I write about Papa's clandestine affair? Aunt Sarah, my greatest champion, was an alcoholic. How do I deal with the time old Uncle Harry came on to me? (If they would be hurt, leave it out, fictionalize it, or refer to "a relative" or "someone close to me.") How do I find time to write when I'm holding down two jobs? Was self-confidence or self-seeking the real reason I left home, changed jobs, or lovers? I never gave my marriage enough hard thought. (Figure it out as best you can right now. An autobiography is an unfinished story.)

You've filled the wastebasket many times with crumpled papers trying to get past page one. You think what you've written is awkward or dull. Organizing the stuff is too much. Writing is too hard. Too lonely.

These problems can be faced and solved a step at a time. Mere desire can give way to decision, decision to determination. When you feel ready to begin, the ideas must be trained to

1

proceed from your head, down your arm to your fingers and pen, along those awesome blank pages.

I'll suggest guidelines, exercises, and mechanics of craft for those unschooled in book writing. Even some of you who are schooled can profit from new angles, information, and tools.

Maybe you just need more courage. The favorite all-round cop-out is, "Who wants to hear about Little Me?" The best beginning is that *you* do. Your life is worthy of being a book.

The second greatest block is fear of literary comparison. The rule for this is: don't be afraid to write badly at first. You may be a perfectionist who expects to sit down at a piano the first time you see one and dash off a sonata. This actually means your self-esteem is in trouble. There's a skill to building it. Self-esteem extends to your place in society. Your life experiences, needs, feelings, thoughts, ideas, opinions, and discoveries are a part of history. You have a role in molding the *zeitgeist* (spirit of the times) that forewarns major social changes.

The better you understand your life and tell about it, the better future generations will understand the development of civilization.

You may think, "Who cares?" to all this. "I just want to tell my story. I'm not concerned with history or humanity. I don't even have a definite reason. That's all right. Reasons may develop along the way. I promise you won't be the same person at the end of this project.

If you need more courage to write, it will grow from self-respect———▶writing———▶more self-respect———▶more writing. Don't procrastinate. Learn as you go.

There is a variety of reasons why people have written their stories. Most fit three broad categories: family heritage, self-examination, and publication and profit. But you can cross-fertilize these, mold them into new shapes, and invent your own. The special ingredient in your story can't be duplicated. Some people discover their reason after the book is written.

Anaïs Nin, the popular diarist, wrote:

> By beginning a diary, I was already conceding that life would be more bearable if I looked at it as an adventure and a tale. I was telling myself the story of a life, and this transmutes into an adventure the things that shatter you.

Somerset Maugham said about *Of Human Bondage*, his famous autobiographical novel:

> This book did for me what I wanted, and when it was issued to the world ... I found myself free forever of those pains and unhappy recollections. I put into it everything I knew, and having at last finished it, I prepared to make a new start.

Gloria Swanson vowed that her autobiography would tell all:

> Age, if nothing else, entitles me to set the record straight before I dissolve. I've given my memoirs far more thought than any of my marriages. You can't divorce a book.

Between extremes of soul-searching and practicality, reasons span a wide range: self-justification; desire for fame; influences that shaped you; what was important to you; services rendered; to credit others with helping you; to tell a group of interesting anecdotes; to highlight and share the most memorable time of your life; the pure joy of storytelling; catharsis; transposing personal experiences into profit; truth seeking; describing human growth and development; the mechanics of achievement as a guide and inspiration to others; the joy of self-discovery and self-knowledge; getting sympathy and understanding from others; to find hope or direction; to stimulate a search for the missing parts of your life; to put the pieces of your life together; search for identity; to achieve immortality through writing yourself as a character in a play; to feel better about yourself; to make peace with the past. And there is always the motive of revenge—best executed in fiction form!

All these reasons are from actual books. No literary law declares that motives be lofty. Even a master diarist like Samuel Pepys wrote more to entertain himself and others than to inform or educate. However, the instruction comes through. All writing is exposure of one sort or another.

Creative expression is a valid reason in itself. Another impulse is pure nostalgia. A delicious warmth of memories comes over us—of a time when we felt intensely good, or just felt intensely. We can percolate emotional depths long submerged, reminders of our neglected repertory of feelings. Bathing a numbed heart in good feelings can heal psychic wounds and restore the sense of being fully alive.

John Holt, an outstanding educator and author, recently wrote about a personal experiment. In this autobiographical writing, he gives a unique reason:

> If I could learn to play the cello well, I could show by my own example that we all have greater powers than we think; that whatever we want to learn to do, we probably can learn; that our lives and our possibilities are not determined and fixed by what happened to us when we were little, or by what experts say we can or cannot do.

This is an example of how you could describe one episode that exemplifies the meaning of your life.

If there is such a thing as true autobiography, it is this: that you allow us a glimpse of your soul, even if you present a fragment of your life.

There are reasons for not writing autobiography. In these days of avid consumption of spice and venom, there is no holding back anyone who wishes to profit by revealing intimacies without regard for others. There are those, too, who use the art of autobiography as an excuse to peddle an opinion, hide a truth, or embark on a diatribe. There are severe risks in these motives. George Misch, classic scholar of autobiography, warns that "even the cleverest liar, in his prefabricated or embroidered stories about himself, will be unable to deceive us as to his character." If you need to get something out of your system, do it in fiction form.

In order for you to pinpoint your reasons for writing an autobiography, it may help to consider some reasons why people read them. What's the fascination? Curiosity, of course, but there is more to it. One researcher said that autobiography offers us an unparalleled insight into the mode of consciousness of other men.

Life-styles of others are a way of checking out our own. Are we getting the most out of life or a particular part of it? How did *they* achieve success? What made *her* appealing to those movie stars she married? What is it like to raise a handicapped child?

One autobiographer claimed she didn't read anyone else's work so it would not "come through" her own. But I see nothing wrong with reading others for ideas and inspiration. You'll come through your work, anyway. If you have not read many autobiographies, start dipping into the various genres. Among my favorites are *My Several Worlds* by Pearl S. Buck; *My Memories and Adventures* by Arthur Conan Doyle (creator of Sherlock Holmes); *If Memory Serves* by Sacha Guitry; *Fear of Flying,* a fictional autobiography by Erica Jong; and the recent *Coal Miner's Daughter* by Loretta Lynn, currently a movie.

A major problem that comes up invariably is the tricky business of truth. Which truth or truths? There are many truths —of belief, opinion, outlook, and feeling. How much truth? What has to be left out for reasons ranging from delicacy to threat of libel? When does a half-truth become an untruth?

You may have no difficulty in telling all, being willing or eager to bare your soul. Conversely, autobiography can be a means of hiding the truth. You may want to present a certain public image and carefully select material to support this image. But in some cases, it's what you are *not* in touch with that trips you up. Your story is in danger of being disjointed or full of holes.

But do we know the truth? Can we know it? Is part of it hidden from ourselves? Should we try to dig it all out? This is a personal decision, but beware of becoming preoccupied with knowing and telling the whole truth and nothing but. It can bog you down. You can become enamored of authentic detail. Nothing is wrong with detail if dates, descriptions, and sensory experiences add interest. But when exact detail isn't available, it's permissible to fill in. Keep the story flowing. What is important is the gist of how you perceive yourself, the world, and your relationship to it—your true perception.

Even Margaret Mead, a stickler for detail, wasn't bothered by the embellishments and imagination of her anthropological subjects:

Possibly it isn't quite true that blue eyes in the family came from the one blue-eyed baby who was rescued when the wagon train was attacked by Indians on the Oregon Trail. Somebody's great-great-great-grandfather was saved. He might well have been yours.

Today's openness is partly a reaction against past restrictions and prejudices. Today there are social strata in which one may live safely that accept any mode of life. Risks of reprisal or being socially ostracized are fewer than in the past, with its stigma or stereotypes. You can now have a child out of wedlock, intermarry with any race, be a homosexual and self-disclose with safety. You no longer need to hide your rightful preferences and choices, and you can sell books about them.

But what does self-revelation do for you internally?

O. Hobart Mowrer, pioneer psychologist, makes an argument for the restoration of *exomologesis*, a theological term found only in unabridged dictionaries: "complete openness about one's life, past and present, to be followed by important personal changes, with the support and encouragement of other members of the 'congregation.' "

Mowrer's study traces the loss of this practice through organized religion and its revival in the early Oxford Movement in America. This was a philosophical group founded on right living. It had an important influence on the formation of Alcoholics Anonymous. The founders of AA created a program to be worked at. It includes a moral inventory of oneself, shared with another person, and a system of making amends and correcting errors of thought and behavior.

Exomologesis requires public confession of mistakes and defects, forgiveness of self and others, group support in correcting these wrongs, acceptance into the community, and fellowship for life. In the past, according to Mowrer, it resulted in the ultimate community, where people helped people and everyone was accepted.

Mowrer demonstrates that positive effectiveness of churches and the health of society as a whole rose and fell with this form of openness as a barometer. The connection between honesty and health is borne out by other studies.

William James said:

One would think that in more men the shell of secrecy would have had to open, the pent-in abcess to burst and gain relief, even if the ear that heard the confession were unworthy. The Catholic Church, for obvious utilitarian reasons, has substituted auricular confession to one priest for the more radical act of public confession. We English-speaking Protestants, in the general self-reliance and unsociability of our nature, seem to find it enough if we can take God into our confidence.

There was a closer sense of community in the past, when more extended families were intact. In my mother's oral history the word *sharing* appears over and over. People shared material possessions and they shared their troubles.

For problems of body and mind there was the family doctor. For problems of the soul there was the neighborhood minister, priest, or rabbi. They, too, were among their friends.

Today, we've become accustomed to seek "authorities," usually paid strangers, when we need help. The role of the religious advisor is now paralleled by that of the highly paid psychological therapists who have become a secular priesthood. But the secret disclosed to counselor or confessor is again to be kept secret from the community.

In writing our stories, we have the chance to reveal ourselves not just to another person or a fellowship or even a community, but to the world!

Erik Erikson describes the "identity crisis" as the state in which we have become so successful at hiding from ourselves that we no longer know who we are.

Sidney Jourard, psychologist and researcher, deals with case studies that prove the dire effects of secrecy:

I believe that in the effort to avoid becoming known, a person provides for himself a cancerous kind of stress which is subtle and unrecognized but nonetheless effective in producing not only the assorted patterns of unhealthy personality which psychiatry talks about, but also the wide array of physical ills that have come to be recognized as the stock in trade of psychosomatic medicine.

C. G. Jung, the noted Swiss psychiatrist, confirms this:

> An unconscious secret is more injurious than a conscious one ... to cherish secrets and hold back emotion is a psychic misdemeanor for which nature visits us with sickness.

Self-revelation is often akin to sensationalism these days. People tell all, uncovering the real person behind the public image or screen personality. They offer gossip, telling tales of conversion from debauchery to Buddhism, the fight against drug addiction or *Blind Ambition*.

There must be powerful reasons why, in these times, the public seeks entree into the private lives of others. I believe that what people are looking for, underneath it all, is simply to *feel* more through vicarious experience.

So whether or not you choose to divulge secrets, veil them, imply them, or attack them frontally, telling secrets adds spice to a book, and health to the psyche.

Discretion and caution are necessary if a secret would hurt you or others. Carefully select material you'll feel comfortable and safe to make public.

But there is no need to hold out on yourself. Uncover the deepest truths of your private world through journal writing, meditation, therapy. Don't just guess superficially at the reasons on record why your life took the turnings it did. You'll have a clearer vision as to whether you were a victim or mover of circumstance. Faulty perceptions—the screens through which you view your life—throw truth off the track. They cloud vision of past events with myths, prejudices, emotional colorations, limited or shortsighted experiences, and faded recollections of time.

We don't expect to achieve perfect and whole truth at any time. It is the striving toward its unfolding that counts, and this is a lifetime process.

At the core of self-revelation is unconditional self-acceptance and self-love. Isn't this the way we want it from others? Begin by being your own counselor. Give hard thought to your life's major situations. Rethink your story and write it authentically.

Our negative side, painful experiences, wrong turnings,

lower choices—all become a treasury of material for the autobiography. Whatever they are, they are useful for edification and growth. They are not items for remorse, guilt, shame, and regret. The world we arrive in at birth molds part of us. We finish the job of ordering our lives. When the pieces come together, a mosaic appears, sometimes out of a life of seeming chaos.

During the course of this project, you will see your life as a whole. Every life has a purpose, a plan, a meaning of its own, whether you believe it's your own doing, karmic destiny, socially imposed, or by divine plan.

EXERCISE 1. THE WHEEL OF LIFE _____

PURPOSE OF THIS EXERCISE
In this chapter I spoke of viewing your life as a whole. This exercise enables you to get an initial, quick panoramic view of it. Write quickly, whatever pops into your head—as you see things now.

INSTRUCTIONS
There are five steps. With each step, you will add material to Diagram 1 (see page 10).

STEP 1
Divide the years of your life into seven parts.

Fill in the diagram with your ages and corresponding years —in each of the seven segments.

Leave segment 8 blank for the time being—it's marked "From Now On"—this will be Step 4.

EXAMPLE (A STUDENT):
Julie M's age (in 1981) is forty-four. Her year of birth is 1937.

Forty-four divided by seven will give six years to each segment, with two years left over—add these to the last segment—#7

DIAGRAM 1. THE WHEEL OF LIFE

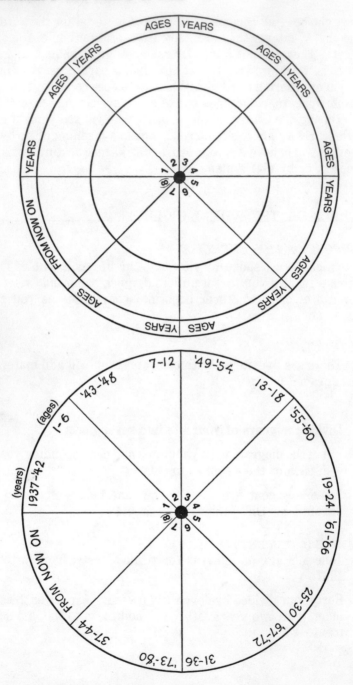

EXAMPLE (JULIE M):

STEP 2 (ADD TO DIAGRAM 1)

Using a word or a short phrase, jot down the major events that occurred during the years in each segment.

Do it fast; don't stop to ponder.

If nothing comes to mind, leave out that segment.

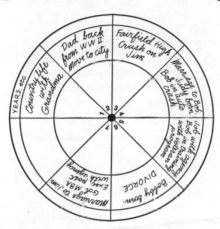

STEP 3 (ADD TO DIAGRAM 1)

Review what you've written for a moment.

Jot down—fast—what kind of period this was—each segment separately—e.g., busy, traumatic, dull.

STEP 4

Using Diagram 2 choose categories that are important in your life and fill in, with just a few words, what you wish to accomplish from now on—in each category.

DIAGRAM 2.

CATEGORY	WISHED-FOR ACCOMPLISHMENTS

EXAMPLE (JULIE M):

CATEGORY	WISHED-FOR ACCOMPLISHMENTS
Social Life	A few close friends. A woman buddy.
Professional	My own agency
Location	A house on the beach
Activities	Travel 2 times a year.
Health	More energy. Lose 6 lbs.
Spiritual	Meditate regularly
Intellectual	More cultural education
Emotional	Better stability. More ups than downs
Psychological	Work out past traumas
Marriage-Family	More time together for fun.

STEP 5

Finally, write down your impressions, realizations, or insights about what you have written in this exercise—thoughts and feelings.

EXAMPLE (JULIE M):

It seemed chaotic and riddled with external blows, but I began to see the part I played in bringing on certain events. I see, too, the responsibilities I need to assume to achieve the goals I outlined.

EXAMPLE (A RETIRED SCHOOLTEACHER):

I was amazed to see that I did so much. I was also amazed to see the highlight of my life was my sabbatical!

EXAMPLE (A SUCCESSFUL LAWYER):

I get a fragmented feeling that bothers me—I think it's because I suddenly became aware of unfinished business during the years fourteen to twenty and between thirty-four and forty.

EXERCISE 2. TURNING POINTS

PURPOSE OF THIS EXERCISE

To see the significant changes in your life—when your life took a turning—from one kind of life to another or from one major event to another.

Doing this exercise can also spark ideas for separate episodes suitable for short stories, articles, or other short pieces. It can help, too, in studying the factors or influences in a life that cause change.

INSTRUCTIONS

There are two steps:

Step 1 will help you sort out what you see as your significant changes.

Step 2 will take one change you didn't like and help you work with it—to get a more positive perspective.

STEP 1

Scanning Diagram 1, make a list of the turning points in your life. Think of personality change, or periods such as marriage, relocation, new job. It can also be a time of shifting from uphill to downhill or vice versa, or an accidental meeting or event.

Comment, if you wish, on one or more of the following:

Was there one special turning point?

Which were internal, that is, when you came to realize something or made a decision?

Which were forced changes or external events?

EXAMPLE (A COLLEGE STUDENT):
STEP 1:

1. Drop out of college to become independent—left home for graphics outfit in New York.

2. Running into Archie on the subway and being offered job in Honolulu.

3. Meeting John at Kay's dinner and almost marrying him

4. Following Gary back to New York.

5. My abortion.

6. Decision to go for career at old agency and return to college for more training.

Comment:
Looking at it this way, it's obvious that I made willful, lame-brained decisions, mostly involving men. I also realize that I attached myself to male artists, taking second place and avoiding my own achievement in art.

STEP 2:
My big negative turning point was my abortion. No way to avoid the fact that it was not accidental. I sabotaged my career opportunity by this move.

If it hadn't been so gruesome and spun my head around, I might still be doing my old number with guys, probably now with Gary and his drug scene.

EXERCISE 3. EPITAPH _____

PURPOSE OF THIS EXERCISE
To get a capsule view of your life and its meaning.

To deal with the subject of death. This will invariably arise in your thoughts as you review your life, so let's get the impact over with.

Repressed and specific fears may emerge which may surprise you. It's important to confront them as soon as possible, or else they may deter you from writing the book.

INSTRUCTIONS
Using the third-person or objective point of view, compose your own epitaph as you would wish to have it carved on your tombstone. It can be a large tombstone.

Make a positive statement about the latter part of your life.

Write the year of your birth, death, and what you died of. (You may prefer to mark a question mark for this.)

If you're stuck, use one or more of the following guides:

What kind of life has it been in general—uphill, smooth going, or a mixture?

Straight line to a goal or many turnings?

Contribution to the world.

What were you good at? Expert at?

How do you wish to be remembered?

EXAMPLE (A SEVENTY-TWO-YEAR-OLD WOMAN):
She was a battler, and her concern was for the underdog. She was a good wife, daughter, cook, and homemaker. Her

co-workers found her understanding and giving, and gave in return a good measure of love. She was born in 1906 and died in 1984—dropped dead on the golf course.

EXAMPLE (A DOCTOR):
He was a mixed bag. His life was fragmented until he found his life's work and learned to take the rest of it with a lighter touch. He died in 2000, age seventy, of sexual exhaustion.

EXERCISE 4. SECRETS _____

PURPOSE OF THIS EXERCISE
This is to help you begin thinking about which secrets to reveal, how to reveal them, and, especially, how they relate to the flow of your story.

INSTRUCTIONS
There are four steps. They deal with sorting out secrets, choosing one to practice with, putting it in the context of the story, then purging bad feelings about it so that you can write about it without inhibitions.

STEP 1
List your secrets under the following categories:

1. Deep and dark secrets there is no way you are willing to disclose.

2. Those you might consider telling if you could find the right way.

3. Important information for your story, but which you would prefer to veil.

4. Those you would tell, but since they involve someone else, you're not sure how the other person would react. You don't want to hurt anyone's feelings or be sued.

5. Those you are ready to tell.

EXAMPLE (A DIVORCED WOMAN):

1. (Deep, dark.) The time I pretended to feel ill and stayed in my friend's apartment while she went out in order to find and read letters from her boyfriend. I was in love with him too.

2. (Might tell—the right way.) The time I got drunk with C and let him take nude photos of me.

3. (Important information—but to veil.) My best friend's husband made a play for me and I rejected him. It would hurt her to know this, but is important to my story at that time.

4. (Involve someone else.) What a coward N was to walk out on me the way he did.

5. (Ready to tell.) I need to explain M's behavior that created a rift, but I discovered it was because he takes drugs.

STEP 2

If you left out specific data, would your story lack continuity, meaning, or impact, or become disjointed?

EXAMPLE (A WRITER):

I have to find a way of disclosing the fact that my sister sabotaged my job search, forcing me to leave town or confront her. Without a definite reason, leaving town would seem like another "geographical cure" for my struggles at the time.

STEP 3

Choose a secret you are ready to tell and write a sentence at the crucial moment of experience.

EXAMPLE (A NINETEEN-YEAR-OLD STUDENT):

Should I? Shouldn't I? Wally's term paper had gotten him an A last semester and he pressed it on me to turn in as my own. It would give us more time together, was his reasoning. Our friends knew and urged me to use it—it was the "in" thing, anyway. I wanted so badly to be "in," to get a good grade, and to live with Wally. I took the paper. I would have to live with this act because I wanted to live with Wally more.

STEP 4

Choose a secret concerning something you did and for which you feel guilty. Then make a list of items under the heading "I forgive myself because:".

EXAMPLE (A WOMAN EXECUTIVE):

I have been carrying a load of guilt now for twelve years because Karen died of a heart attack in my office, I thought, because of my negligence. She was my best employee and a friend.

I forgive myself because:
1. Karen begged me not to call the paramedics.

2. I hadn't been aware of her illness.

3. I did all I could at the moment.

4. When the medics came, they said it wouldn't have made a difference if they had arrived sooner.

5. Only God has the power of life and death. Karen's time had come. I was not the cause.

READINGS

BATES, E. STUART. *Inside Out: An Introduction to Autobiography.* New York: Sheridan House, 1937. A large, comprehensive study of autobiographers within the author's own categories: e.g., poor folk, religion, wrong turnings, work, childhood.

BURR, ANNA ROBESON. *The Autobiography: A Critical and Comparative Study.* Cambridge, Mass.: Houghton Mifflin Co., 1909. Two hundred and sixty autobiographies are covered in this remarkable and detailed account of the field. A must for the scholar. The author presents her own categories: e.g., self-esteem, humor, genius, character.

FRANKLIN, BENJAMIN. *The Autobiography of Benjamin Franklin.* New York: A.S. Barnes & Co., 1944. One of the great classics. Basic for the autobiographer interested in being well organized. The style is simple and free.

HOLT, JOHN. *Never Too Late.* New York: Delacorte Press, 1978. An unusual, enlightening study of the learning process by a brilliant educator. Encouraging for those with lack of self-confidence.

JOURARD, SIDNEY M. *The Transparent Self.* Princeton, N.J.: D. Van Nostrand Co., 1964. One of the basic popular works in psychology, dealing with honesty and openness with ourselves and others.

JUNG, CARL GUSTAV. *Memories, Dreams, and Reflections.* New York: Pantheon Books, 1963. Jung's autobiography, one of the great studies, and easy to read. A marvel of self-honesty and self-understanding.

KEEN, SAM, and FOX, ANNE VALLEY. *Telling Your Story: A Guide to Who You Are and Who You Can Be.* New York: Doubleday & Co., 1973. A small book, suggesting how to get in touch with yourself through Esalen-type exercises.

PADOVER, SAUL K. *Confessions and Self-Portraits: 4600 Years of Autobiography.* New York: The John Day Co., 1957. Selections from seventy-five autobiographies, with comments. A wonderful and scholarly work with an opportunity to sample the flavors of some outstanding personalities.

PASCAL, ROY. *Design and Truth in Autobiography.* London: Routledge & Kegan Paul, 1960. One of the most-referred-to classic texts about the craft of autobiography, from the author's standards of excellence. Purist in viewpoint but broadly informative in its detailed study of the various aspects of autobiography.

PORTER, ROGER J., and WOLF, H. R. *The Voice Within.* New York: Alfred A. Knopf, 1973. A well-written and thoughtful perspective on excerpts from the works of twenty-one autobiographers according to subjects, e.g., work, self-knowledge. Studious comments precede each example.

WETHERED, H. N. *The Curious Art of Autobiography.* New York: Philosophical Library, 1956. A basic research text about the worlds of twenty-one renowned autobiographers from the sixteenth through the twentieth centuries. Critiques are intermixed with excerpts dealing with autobiographical forms from a scholarly viewpoint. Opinionated as to "true" autobiography, but very useful in studying details of the craft.

2

History, Autobiography, and You

Few will have the greatness to bend history itself, but each of us can work to change a small portion of events, and in the total of all those acts will be written the history of this generation.

—ROBERT KENNEDY

There are missing pages in American history—yours. Historians need them to complete the story of our times. People of all kinds will need to surface.

Many schoolbooks still have us visualizing history mostly through its famous men. But hidden material is emerging, especially since the genealogy craze has reached a point of high intensity.

In 1977, Alex Haley's *Roots* was aired in an innovative television form—on eight consecutive nights. The response was phenomenal: the audience ranged from 64 million to 81 million (on the final night) as word-of-mouth enthusiasm escalated. It was the largest audience in television history. Blacks and whites both were psychologically shaken by the specter of one part of America's shadow side of history. A news editor said that it "gave personality to a faceless past about which most American blacks—not to mention whites—knew next to nothing."

The genealogy bug caused a roots-fever epidemic. The National Archives in Washington reported over 5,000 letters a week

requesting information about how to trace ancestors. Classes
and clubs multiplied in record numbers. It became the top hobby
in the country.

But even before Haley's book appeared, genealogy was the
third-ranking hobby, cutting across ethnic lines.

The television series *Holocaust* did for the Jews what *Roots*
did for the blacks as the whole country was awakened to the
reality of a chilling period of history the last generation was only
vaguely aware of.

Interest in genealogy is not purely ethnic. The histories of
art, science, and other fields are being expanded. Sister Nancy
Fierro, a pianist-composer at Immaculate Heart College in Los
Angeles, is finding her roots researching piano works by women
composers from the eighteenth and nineteenth centuries.

Women were discouraged from serious professional study
by publishers, families, and society in general. Still, a surprising
number composed operas, sonatas, polonaises, and other works.
Some achieved acclaim in their time. Most were forgotten after
their deaths. Sister Fierro says:

> Enlightened mediocrity was encouraged. Women were ex-
> pected to become proficient enough to delight company, to
> perform an afternoon musicale.
>
> So far, our combined efforts have uncovered about
> 1,000 women composers from the 18th and 19th centuries.

As you begin to view your life in its historical setting and
ally yourself with your times, your story will accrue more scope
and power. Historical background material is of enormous use
for understanding yourself and others, and for deciding how to
best work out your story in these times.

Autobiography as a form developed in relationship to history.

Just what is autobiography? The word is composed of three
Greek ones: *autos*—"self," *bios*—"life," and *graphia*—"writing." But the word itself seems to defy definition. Types overlap,
refuse to fit molds, and are sometimes confined to specialties.
Even determined scholars are hard put to pin them down. They
categorize them loosely and criticize them against what each
considers "true autobiography." No two definitions agree. It's

not even accurate to say that autobiography is an account of one's inner and/or outer life, or a portion of a life to date, by the person himself: some life stories are "as told to" other writers; Guy de Maupassant's "La Horla" is about his future; Jean-Paul Sartre wrote an autobiography *up to* the age of twelve; and the Swiss poet Carl Spitteler wrote his story ending when he was four!

Let's avoid rigid labels and standards. By simply calling it your story, you are free to tell it any way that feels good to you.

On the other hand, a story needs some shape and identity so that the reader understands what kind of book it is.

There is such a variety of ways to tell your story that you may get confused unless you are very clear about which is best for the project you have in mind.

Between complex theories and no theory at all, I've worked out a simple list of basic categories for autobiographical writing to simplify the work in this book. See where your story idea fits in. It may overlap several categories, but the important point is emphasis—what your story is *mostly* about:

1. *Family record.* Includes family history. May include comments about relatives and events. Focus is on *family*.

2. *Panoramic or chronological autobiography or life review.* Necessary if your goal is self-examination. From birth to present. Focus is on *your* life.

3. *Partial autobiography.* This type deals with a special part of your life or a significant episode. Contact with another person may be the most memorable. Focus is on *your relationship* to a person or event.

4. *Thematic autobiography.* Although all stories have a point of view, you may want to use a *specific point of view* as the focus. In this category I include the following:

   a. *The memoir.* Usually deals with your thoughts and feelings about another person, a group, a point in time, a setting or environment that is either physical (e.g., country life in Connecticut in the early thirties) or a political arena (worked in the Pentagon during Kennedy's term). The focus is *on the other* with yourself in the background in a minor role—as an observer.

b. *The portrait.* Presenting the substance and/or essence of someone you knew, or have researched. Usually concrete, i.e., built with factual data.

c. *The reminiscence, meditation, recollection, or reflection.* Usually deals with feelings about something or someone, deep thoughts, insights.

d. *Confession, revelation, apologia.* How you changed, came to realize something.

e. *Essay.* A point of view about a specific subject or issue, with strong material to support or defend it.

5. *Short nonfiction pieces.* Anything—such as self-help or travel adventures. Something interesting you did or learned—to share with the reader. This differs from the thematic in that it is concerned with subjects rather than themes—themes referring mostly to a philosophical statement, a universal concept. Themes and subjects may, however, overlap.

6. *Fictionalized autobiography or dramatized diary.* Anything about your life you want to (or have to) transpose to fiction. Here you can develop a personal philosophy—anonymously—through a character in a novel, novelette, short story, mood piece, character study, stage or screen play, or television play (new forms of the latter are being developed continuously).

7. *Miscellaneous and special autobiographical writings.* Poetry, humor, impressionistic or abstract forms.

Autobiography is expressed by more than the written word. Painting, architecture, photography, academic theses—all have personal statement and style.

In Rembrandt's sixty-two self-portraits, he seemed to be exploring himself from different aspects and to penetrate the canvas.

In the forties, Toyo Miyatake, a photographer held in an American internment camp for Japanese-Americans, made a "photographic diary." It is the only visual record of our deplorable treatment of the Japanese-Americans during World War II.

Scholars of the historical development of autobiography set personal and diverse standards of proper forms against which every work is compared. Many agree that the first true autobiography was Saint Augustine's *Confessions,* written in the fourth century, and that this form disappeared from the literary scene and did not appear again until a thousand years later. One of the researchers insists that "there remains no doubt that the autobiography is essentially European." This is an example of what I mean by rigid parameters.

I believe personal experiences, recorded in any way, are "true." Autobiographical information throughout the ages is a continuous, uninterrupted process, molding itself to the mores and traditions of changing civilizations.

Can we discount the cave dweller's drawing on the rocky walls of his home, documenting a hunting feat? By his style, we can feel his personality.

People have always recorded their stories, many in secrecy. The desire to avoid oblivion is basic.

The *griot* or male storyteller of Africa did not have a monopoly on oral history. Stories were passed down through women—in fact, Alex Haley's first clue came from a memory held by his oldest living female relative. But it's interesting to note that "old wives' tales" suggest fabrication!

If you train your eye, you'll realize that personal stories are everywhere. Take the Bible. The story of Job is unique in its message, its intricacy of form. The anonymous author, a poetic dramatist, leaves no doubt as to Job's being the player through whom he expressed his own character key. Marchette Chute, author and researcher, describes this interplay between the author of Job and Job as the character in the drama:

Job never found what he was looking for. He could not, because his creator, the author of the poem, did not know the answer himself, and had too much integrity to offer a compromise . . . his heart was with the lonely men of God who went out to find reality for themselves, forsaking every intellectual belief and emotional comfort that might hold them back; and in writing the Book of Job he became himself not the least of these.

This is an exceptional example of one principle of the autobiography compared with biography. The autobiography is about a life unfinished, and the author's *ideas* may still be incomplete. Many people wait to write their stories until they feel more "finished" in thought and deed, but the searching, the labor, not just the fruits, are interesting and inspiring. Note Lillian Hellman's *An Unfinished Woman,* one of her autobiographies.

Through the Songs of Solomon we can share the author's tribute to romantic and physical love. In the Psalms, the songs and poetry permit us to touch the heart of others who have suffered, longed, and loved as we have:

My voice shalt thou hear in the morning, O Lord; in the morning will I direct my prayer unto thee, and will look up.

Who can understand his errors? Cleanse thou me from secret faults.

How long wilt thou forget me, O Lord? Forever? How long wilt thou hide thy face from me?

The Lord is my rock, and my fortress, and my deliverer; my God; my strength, in whom I will trust; my buckler, and the horn of my salvation, and my high tower.

These are voices of real people sharing their feelings. They have provided comfort and inspiration for centuries.

Henry David Thoreau said that to look into one another's eyes is a miracle. The same can happen by touching with words —whatever the span of years. This is what is "true" in literature. Communication and the longing to be heard and understood are basic human hungers.

Modes of recording personal accounts reflected the modes of the ages. The ancient Egyptians and Babylonian Assyrians, with stylized art systems, left their personal stories in stylized forms. Stories of the wealthy were told in series of paintings on the walls and ceilings of their tombs. The poor did their best on their few possessions such as pottery.

Tombs were for the transition from this life to another. The life at hand was considered only a chapter in the transmigration of the soul. Complete public records of the individual's life were offered as evidence to the worthiness of the occupant to receive safe and successful passage. Therefore, only positive actions were visible. Their private life was kept secret. Walls and ceilings were covered with illustrated biographies "as told to" hired admirers, accompanied by autobiographical statements of unrestrained self-aggrandizement: "I was the pride of the king's soul." "My praise ascended to the skies."

In Babylonian and Assyrian tombs, cuneiform chronicles attested to the heroic accomplishments of the kings. Their unlimited power was considered divine. They could say whatever they pleased about themselves. Pride in the destruction of the enemy was a favorite subject: "I took them alive and impaled them on stakes." "I dyed mountains like wool with their blood."

But their interior life was not recorded; at least, there is little evidence that autobiographies were written about anyone's whole life.

It wasn't until the classical cultures of Greece and Rome that the self-portrait with self-examination was accepted and encouraged. Still, Aristotle, who set patterns of thought, believed that the ideal man never discusses himself with others. As for women, "Silence is a woman's glory." Biography became a definite form in the search for human perfection, but only a handful of autobiographies have been passed down in both Greek and Roman literature.

The Middle Ages featured morality. The fate of the soul was of primary importance, and divine retaliation was feared for the slightest impurities. At the beginning of this period we find Saint Augustine's *Confessions,* thought to be the first true autobiography. Self-analysis of his inner life tells of his conversion to

Christianity and is "addressed to his maker, not the general public." This was as honest an effort as was found until then. God, by this time in religious concept, could not be duped or persuaded.

But most religious accounts of this age were lopsided in that the outer world seems not to have existed as we read them. We do not get a feeling of background against which these internal dramas were self-observed. From the view of their writers, the material world was of little consequence.

With the Renaissance (fourteenth to sixteenth centuries) came a higher respect for the individual, freedom from conformity, freedom of self-reflection and expression. It opened up another area of appreciation of the autobiography—as a reservoir of psychological and historical data. It was the Golden Age of the autobiography.

In the sixteenth century, artistic achievements or any other efforts in the material world were described. Benvenuto Cellini's romantic, military, and artistic exploits were unashamedly self-appreciative. But Johann Wolfgang von Goethe said that reading Cellini enabled him to visualize the entire century. Because of this freedom of expression, we get a vibrant view of a portion of life as it was. It was a flamboyant century, of both Casanova and Saint Theresa of Avila, both believers in personal missions —to cite contrasts in the extreme!

The seventeenth century was noted for classic memoirs and diaries. It was the age of Samuel Pepys and John Bunyan. Morality with overtones of humor flourished, but Daniel Defoe's *Moll Flanders* was written as pseudofictional autobiography.

Around the eighteenth century, autobiography became recognized as a form with equal stature among other literary forms. Confessionals flourished. Goethe became a student of this form and wrote his own. Johann Gottfried von Herder, German poet-philosopher, prompted some scholars to make a collection of outstanding autobiographies. Charles Gibbon wrote his, as one writer remarked, in the same manner as his epic work, *The Decline and Fall of the Roman Empire.* Many still consider it the mightiest of autobiographical work. Among other highly prized works of this century are autobiographies of Jean-Jacques Rousseau and Benjamin Franklin.

The nineteenth century fully accepted the autobiography as a source of psychological and historical information, and during

riod it was developed at great length and depth. On this
tion Charles Darwin, Charles Lamb, and Thomas De
Quincey produced their stories.

In our own century, autobiographies are being written at an
accelerated pace and the public devours them ravenously. But
we have been trained to believe that authorities and sparkling
personalities know more than we do. Idolatry rules the day, and
we follow the antics of movie stars, jet-setters, rock stars, and
political leaders with the same passion that people in other times
followed gods, prophets, and philosophers. In former times, autobiography had a moral, instructive purpose. Now its purpose
is manufactured by the media. I call this *vicarious esteem.* It is
not mentally or emotionally healthy. It stunts our growth
through taking on someone else's identity instead of developing
our own.

This is why I wish more "common" people would write their
stories. In our problem-ridden culture our answers will come
from within, but not without an exploration of the social and
psychological background of our age.

Eleanor Roosevelt wrote a series of autobiographies using
herself as a camera eye to open to the reader the political scene
during the Roosevelt era. More recently Betty Ford, in her story,
gave us a glimpse of the same arena from a more personal view:
the glamour and demands of being First Lady and how they
affected "an ordinary woman who was called onstage at an extraordinary time."

Nearly all of the Watergate group have written about their
points of view.

What about another level of historical view—that of the
average person, thrown against the changes of his time, unable
to move history as it is possible to do from a top position?

I urge you to adopt a position of power, not powerlessness.
Maybe we can't move history as they do, but we can do it collec-
tively.

By studying your life, you will find your personal and social
sources of power. You can become an active participant in historical progress.

Here's a demonstration of how a personal story is woven
into its historical background, and how you can learn more about
yourself this way.

A student's summary about herself:

> I am a: divorced woman; widow; older woman; worker; teacher; Jew; consumer; mother; daughter; Californian; urban dweller.

In writing her story she has a choice of themes:

1. An older woman returning to college.

2. Tragedies and triumphs searching for love.

3. Spiritual awakening and growth by overcoming obstacles.

4. Giving up a career in music to become a teacher.

To choose a theme, she considers the following:

1. What is the most important thing in my life?

2. What forces have been the strongest?

3. What do I want to communicate to my readers so they will understand me?

4. How will all this hold the reader's interest?

She develops a story germ:

> A young widow seeking identity finds it through her work, but falls in love along the way to success. She gives up her work and pours her creative energy into her husband's career. He becomes successful and leaves her. She returns to work. Her goal is merely to make a living to support herself and small son. Her identity is now through motherhood.

Until this point, the story could take place in almost any age or place. But environmental forces begin to erupt within the boring plot suggested above. Here is a turning the story can take:

She has been living as if frozen in the forties and fifties, the years when she was a young girl. When her son reaches his teens, the sixties strike with their psychedelic impact and shake up this little family. It catapults her into the present. Divorce forces her to become involved with the issues of the day—the women's movement, drugs, crime.

She learns to survive and find some joy in life. She does not escape to a cave or a mountain top, or try to stand in the center of the cyclone, undisturbed and serene. She learns to weave in and out of the turbulence. Her identity is now her unfolding self—and the story will be about how she accomplished this.

In writing that seed plot, the student learned:

I had submerged my identity for fear I was not important, or that I would fail, or because the world out there was too intimidating. But when I was forced to face that world, I discovered a resource of strength I didn't know I had.

She could have chosen a simple story of a woman betrayed, or a poor widow's struggle to raise a child, or an older woman's search for love. But these are hackneyed themes unless they take on the issues of historical perspective, as we live it or write it. The powerful significance of the fifties through the seventies, and the way the sweeping social changes affected *one human being in depth,* makes the "ordinary" quite extraordinary.

There is an increasing recognition and appreciation of stories of the nonfamous. A reviewer said about a woman's story:

. . . a poignant book, another in the new wave of books about obscure though sometimes far from ordinary people who have been witnesses to the turbulence of history.

I have come across many cavalier statements such as "The best autobiographies are by men and women of outstanding achievement in life," and "A sincere, full autobiography is not written save by important men." The trend today obviously belies these old attitudes.

History told through and about famous people has led us down the garden path and given us a distorted view.

In Amsterdam, Henk Jan Gortzak is rewriting the history of colonial Holland. He talked with people in Third World countries and those who actually lived in Dutch colonies, and studies anthropological material. A reviewer said of Gortzak's work, "The picture with which he emerged is a savage contrast to the history taught in the schools."

At least one fellow took the bull by the horns: Bradley Reed Smith, private citizen. He became upset at the world out there because, he said, "It was not the way I wanted things to be." The issues were "too large to handle," and he wanted to "have a way of understanding it." He gave up his apartment, moved back "with Mommy," and published *Smith's Journal*. He felt his ideas were worth expressing:

> They would only have a place as something coming from a real person, a real life, an ordinary person . . . it occurred to me that I could express my fancy ideas if I also put in all of the lowdown stuff from my diary. I could show the real person and then say, look at this, these are my ideas. If I have them, you can, too. You don't have to be an expert to think clearly about an issue.

In 1965, during the Panamanian riots, Smith realized how much the news was affecting his life. He offers his ideas about practically everything now in his journal. One of his "fancy ideas" at the end of 1978 was that revolutionaries, in the name of the people, usually brutalize the people: "It took a symbiotic, collaborative action by Somoza and the Sandinistas (in Nicaragua) to pincer the public."

He keeps his project alive with part-time jobs and full-time dedication. Is it worth it? He says:

> It is a way to prove I am alive. It is a way of being connected to experience. It is a way to find significance in ordinary life.

EXERCISE 1. REASONS _____

PURPOSE OF THIS EXERCISE
To narrow down ideas for your story, background or setting, and theme. How to fuse these elements.

INSTRUCTIONS
In one sentence, give a reason for writing your story in relation to the following three categories:

1. *Personal.* Your own adventure, struggles, successes. One specific story idea. (Who is telling the story?)

2. *Social.* Where do you fit in as a historical unit? Which group? For example, ethnic, age, sex, religious, work force. (To whom will this story appeal?)

3. *Theme.* The link to universal issues, ideas, etc. Your feelings—and the statement you want to make. (What is it about?)

EXAMPLE (A COLLEGE STUDENT):
1. *Personal.* My romantic struggles with male students as a young female student.

2. *Social.* As a student at an immense California university —student's view of life.

3. *Theme.* To show how many young intellectual men are confused and threatened by women's social transitions at this time, and how this affects the women.

EXAMPLE (A WIDOW IN HER SEVENTIES):
1. *Personal.* The story of my life centered around my marriage. How it changed when my husband died.

2. *Social.* A widow, suddenly cut off from her former friends in the "married world," finds her way to an older singles world.

3. *Theme.* To show the reasons, mechanics, and effects of ageism in our society.

EXERCISE 2. IF I HADN'T BEEN BORN _____

PURPOSE OF THIS EXERCISE

In 1946 there was a movie called *It's a Wonderful Life* with James Stewart—about a man who is about to commit suicide. He is rescued by his guardian angel who turns back the clock, and shows him what his part of the world would have been like if he had never been born. The man learns to appreciate the positive effects he has had on the people in his life and to recall his special contributions to society.

The purpose here is just that. Become aware of how your presence on earth influenced people individually and society in general.

INSTRUCTIONS

Choose three people whose lives you have touched. Write a paragraph or two fantasizing what their lives might have been like if you had never existed. *Deal only with positive factors.*

EXAMPLE (A WOMAN FILMMAKER):

1. *My mother.* She would have opened a dress shop and would have left my father. She never would have had contact with the theater. Her creative abilities in dance, drama, and costume, would never have been realized. Both she and my father might have been lonely. In later years they developed a great marriage.

2. *One of my students.* Would have abandoned playwriting and gone back to Nebraska, joining his father as a milk farmer and believing himself a failure.

3. *My ex-lover.* He would have spent many years with a psychiatrist and struggled with his problems of love and sex. He would have been promiscuous, and might never have learned about a rich and profound relationship with a woman, as he has one now—though it isn't with me.

EXERCISE 3. HOW I SHAPE HISTORY _____

PURPOSE OF THIS EXERCISE

According to what may be called the "domino theory," we influence people and events, and these in turn influence others, and so on. In this exercise, fantasy will go a little farther, to the community and the national, even the international, scene.

INSTRUCTIONS

Choose an incident in which you voted for a candidate, selected a member of an organization, or helped shape or start a group. Fantasize the results of the local and national situation if a different person had been elected. Theorize the impact on history as a chain reaction.

EXAMPLE (A VOLUNTEER LADY):

I helped to elect a dynamite director for a foster child program. With her increased activity, over two hundred children lived to productive adulthood.

If the other candidate—a corrupt politician—had been elected, these children might have died.

This program was a model for many more, helping people become aware that what happens at the other end of the world is important.

EXERCISE 4. CENTRAL CHARACTER _____

PURPOSE OF THIS EXERCISE

With this exercise, you will get the feeling of being the hero or heroine (the central character), and sharpen your perception of his or her personality.

This will also warm up your justification to write your story, as you realize how interesting you are.

INSTRUCTIONS

Choose a character with whom you can identify. This can be out of fiction, history, or real life. It can be one quality or the whole person.

How are the others influenced by this character?
What quality in particular attracts people to him or her?
Can you identify with this quality? Is it a quality you wish you
had or plan to acquire?

EXAMPLE (A SCHOOLTEACHER, MALE):

For many years I have identified with a World War II flying
ace, member of the Flying Tigers. He is dashing, brave, and
more concerned with a cause than himself. He has total confidence and knows exactly what he wants.

I identify in this way: I am confident as a teacher, and more
concerned about my students and their welfare than my job. I'm
a small hero to them in a way.

EXAMPLE (AN ARTIST):

I definitely identify with Gauguin. He took the big risk—
to find a way to really paint.

I wish I had the guts to do the same. If I had a brain in
my head I'd sail off to an island and paint what I feel.

READINGS

AUGUSTINE, SAINT. *Confessions.* Translated by Julie Kernan. New
York: Doubleday & Co., 1962. Wonderfully written, a profound
and honest outpouring of a man addressing God. Advanced in form
for its time. Every serious student should read it.

BUNYAN, JOHN. *The Autobiography of a Soul.* Edited by E. Venables
and M. Peacock. Oxford: Oxford University Press, 1925. The
seventeenth-century religious writer gives an account of his conversion from "a wicked life," i.e., a love of sport, dancing, bell-
ringing, and a game called "tip-cat."

CASANOVA, JACQUES. *The Memoirs of Jacques Casanova.* New York:
Macmillan, 1962. This needs no introduction except that it's a marvelous picture of other activities of the sixteenth century aside
from sex.

CELLINI, BENVENUTO. *The Autobiography of Benvenuto Cellini.* Garden City, N.Y.: Doubleday & Co., 1946. The great sixteenth-cen-
tury artist and adventurer left a stunning account of his times.
Goethe said that by reading it he could envisage the whole of the
sixteenth century.

CHUTE, MARCETTE. *The Search for God.* New York: E. P. Dutton, 1958. A beautifully written book which brings the autobiographical material of the Bible close to home.

DARWIN, CHARLES. *The Autobiography of Charles Darwin.* New York: Harcourt, 1958. One of the most notable and referred-to autobiographical works by the naturalist, who was also a fine writer.

DEAN, JOHN W., III. *Blind Ambition: The White House Years.* New York: Simon & Schuster, 1976. One of the best examples of a hybrid autobiography, a study of a historical background and a partial and thematic type of work, which also comes across as a sort of confession.

DE QUINCEY, THOMAS. *Confessions of an English Opium Eater.* Jacksonville, FL: Heritage House, 1950. Interesting for a historical view of the drug scene and how it affected one human being—and his analysis of his own addiction. It also has philosophical overtones relating to the social scene of the times.

GIBBON, EDWARD. *Memoirs of My Life.* New York: Funk & Wagnall's Co., 1969. The man who wrote *The Decline and Fall of the Roman Empire* wrote his own story in the manner of a great historian. Considered the finest work of its kind by many authorities.

HALEY, ALEX. *Roots.* Garden City, N.Y.: Doubleday & Co., 1976. If you haven't read this by now, do read it for a wonderful example of the meaning of roots and family history. He filled in where facts were missing.

MISCH, GEORGE. *A History of Autobiography in Antiquity.* Cambridge, Mass.: Harvard University Press, 1951. A fascinating and thorough study of the autobiography in early history, peppered with anecdotes, quotes, details. A must for the serious student.

PASCAL, ROY. *Design and Truth in Autobiography.* See Readings, Chapter 1, for notes.

ROOSEVELT, ELEANOR. *This I Remember.* New York: Harper & Bros., 1949. Also *On My Own.* New York: Harper & Bros., 1958.; *The Autobiography of Eleanor Roosevelt,* Harper & Row, 1961. A wonderful and special example of how to write autobiography as a series during different periods of one's life. She writes with charm and honesty, but biographers filled in later those events she couldn't include for reasons of politics, personal modesty, and pain.

ROUSSEAU, JEAN-JACQUES. *Confessions.* Baltimore: Penguin Books, 1954. The eighteenth-century French-Swiss philosopher and influential writer of his century. His life was dramatic and the autobiography, written eight years prior to his death, covers most of the highlights.

SAINT THERESA OF AVILA. *The Way of Perfection.* Translated by Cohen. London: Penguin Books, 1957. The Spanish nun and mystic of the sixteenth century. A story of an intense spiritual seeker and her emotional turbulence and struggle to reform the Carmelite order.

3

When You Were Young

We are not born all at once,
but by bits. The body first,
and the spirit later

—MARY ANTIN,
The Promised Land

Eastern philosophy regards life as a seamless unity. Why then separate youth from adulthood in this study? Childhood years require special handling. In many cases, the further back in memory, the more events are likely to be faded or distorted by what happened between then and now.

Distancing is often deliberate, to avoid painful memories, or used as a mechanical device to select what we need from the stored input in our brain's computer. If we remembered and felt all our experiences all the time, our heads would explode.

There are natural experiences such as learning to walk and talk. Then there is *programming*, or what others feed into us to get us to do what they want us to think, feel, or do. One psychologist says:

> When the five-year-old manfully strides up the walk on that celebrated first day of kindergarten, he takes along with him about 25,000 hours of dual tape recording. One set is his Parent. The other, his Child. He also has a magnificent computer that can click off responses and produce brilliant

ideas by the thousands, *if* it is not totally involved in working out the problems of the NOT O.K.

Examine attitudes through which you perceive the past. Was something I did as a child good or bad? Right or wrong? Did it really happen that way? Did it happen at all, or am I filling in? Is the real Me remembering the event, or is it the Not O.K. Me? Or the Not Me, but someone I'm "supposed to be"?

A common problem of autobiographers is being caught in the crossfire between psychological and sociological theories. There are significant points of change in human development, their interpretation depending on which scientific paper you read. A news item says:

Child development theorists are dissatisfied people. They are not content with existing explanations of how a child grows up, so they engage in the search for more adequate ones. These theories range from early views, such as the Puritan's "sinful and obstinate" child, Rousseau's "moral and curious child," to popular "common-sense" views and the contemporary perspectives of the sociobiologists, psychoanalysts, linguists, behaviorists, and others.

You are told that a "normal" child fits certain labeled grids. Did you? You worry if you didn't. This or that was "inappropriate for my age." You were rewarded or punished then, and you continue to judge yourself, often according to obsolete ideas. Autobiographers tend to defend or excuse "deviant" behavior of the past relevant to "stages."

Take all this lightly and choose what fits your situation. The moment you tap accumulated guilt about past performance, you're setting up obstacles in your goal of present performances, one of which is to *write*.

Your childhood may or may not be the best starting point for you. It depends on how you feel about it and its relevance to the story you choose to tell.

Youth may be wasted on the young, as George Bernard Shaw said, but it's even wasted on the old—if not viewed in true perspective. People often tell me they had terrible childhoods. When they reenter early periods with effective tools, they unearth many happy experiences. Photographs are reexamined and the subjects are often surprised to see themselves smiling and happy during a time they had tried to forget because of associated pain. They now discover it wasn't *all* painful.

It's not unusual for youth revisted to be stripped of a smoky film of nostalgia and warped memories. Emotions rooted in the past we water and tend like herb gardens. We make-believe something happened differently from the way it did. Childhood fantasies can be remembered as real events.

You can write about childhood now as you see it now, or you can gain a new perspective by taking a second look and having second thoughts. If you're doing this project for self-examination, this step is essential. The "real me" in autobiography is usually a literary construct. Most people hang on to a single emotional impression of their childhood: good, bad, sad, happy, miserable. Reality is a mixture of these.

Child-development theories state that emotions are more intense when we are young. Nothing can be compared with our first love, our first trip to the beach.

Paralleling emotional perspective is physical perspective. The child is simply smaller. Childhood places look smaller now. The giant apple tree you used to climb is an ordinary-sized one. But if you look at it through the mind's eye of *your child at that time,* it will feel the same and not disappoint you.

Edwin Muir, the naturalist, never lost his feelings for nature that children have in common. In his life story he says the child "is closer to things, since his eyes are only two or three feet from the ground, not five or six. Grass, stones, insects are twice as near to him as they will be after he has grown up." Muir describes his impressions of his father's breeches and the feeling of burying his face in his mother's skirts as most vivid.

Work on recalling the feelings that accompanied events. These are your feelings, and your reader may not identify with *your* events, but you will evoke their feelings to fit *their* events. Try to catch these feelings in the language of children, less dependent on words. There is an emotional commonality among children: the wonder of the world, the joy of living. When you write about how your adventures felt to you, readers will be reminded of things they had forgotten.

Whether you view your childhood through rose-colored glasses or through a glass darkly, tell it as you see it now. If you change your mind, you can tell it both ways. They are both your truths. But the *way* you tell it will let the reader know more about your mind than will the accuracy and details of what you describe.

But don't be bound by this, either. Carl Spitteler, the Swiss poet, at fifty-two years of age recalled a striking image of animals on a farm he had visited when he was four. There were "rabbits with blue necks, red tails and ears, hens with white and green feet, and little pigs all colors." He distrusted his own memory until he learned later in life that the farmer liked to paint his animals!

Children see things as prettier than they appear to adults. That old apple tree doesn't seem as gorgeous and wonderful as it did when you were four. But maybe kids see the true nature of things more clearly than do jaded grown-ups. One of the rewards you'll find in the actual writing is the thrill of recapturing past moments of joy.

The categories of life vary with individuals. For example, money may be important to someone, the most important thing to another, and insignificant to another.

Two little girls asked:

"Mommy, are we rich or poor?"

"We're not rich. We're not poor."

"What are we then?"

"We're just right. We have enough money to buy the things we want."

One grew up to be a fast earner and fast spender. The other earns slowly but hangs onto it. Money was important, but not a major factor in their lives.

Categories shift around in importance. A fifty-five-year-old woman was suddenly thrust into a hostile job market, unexpectedly and unprepared. At that point, it became a major category for a while.

To spark your memory and imagination, here are some categories that have influenced most autobiographers.

PLACE

Paul Tournier, the psychiatrist-philosopher, said:

> A man becomes attached to his place, he becomes one with it. It becomes a part of his person, of his inner self, so that anything that happens to his place also affects his person.

Place—home—homeland—are visceral images. It is as though we grew from a spot on earth and to be transplanted meant losing some basic nutrients. Some people are uprooted too soon, some too often, and some live as alien corn, struggling to grow in an environment that cannot nourish their specific genus.

One student was forever seeking parks in her cities, craving greenery. Through writing her story, she found that the time she felt most like herself—whole and authentic—was a short period when she ran free in the country. Every student has easily recalled one special place with special meaning and feelings—an attic, a cave, a hideaway in the garage, countryside, a city street, a space under a lakeside tree. Carlos Castaneda elaborates on a three-day search for the exact spot on the floor of the room in which he was to practice his inner odyssey under Don Juan's tutelage.

My mother told me about the public bathhouse at the side of her village in Lithuania, where the children played when it was not being used. The scrubbed wood had a unique aroma. Throughout her life she associated the smell of wood with fun.

Her family all slept in one room with drapes the only attempt at privacy. But she had a private place. Behind the little house, bricks had crumbled on the back wall, leaving a hollow. There she would go off alone to play, arranging little stones in that hollow as a pretend house, train station, or theater. A little peasant girl's imagination was set free in a setting of primitive poverty.

Take time to linger over memories of childhood places in your life. Are they associated with a person or group? Do they stir up special feelings? How did they influence your life? Are you still attached to them?

Did you miss the experience of "place"? Did you move around so much that you didn't get attached to any one place?

Are you a rolling stone? If so, explain how that feels. For those of us who can't go home again, it may offer an alternative.

EARLY EXPERIENCES

Most of us can remember incidents or insights during early childhood that created lifelong patterns of behavior—for better or for worse. One autobiographer invaded his grandfather's cellar when he was three years old and drank himself into unconsciousness. For the rest of his life he despised alcohol.

Children can hate someone easily and get over it quickly. But the French writer Stendhal carried a hate through life. He tells of a tutor he so hated that thirty-five years later he broke off with a girl he was courting because her nose was shaped like the tutor's!

The playwright Sacha Guitry adored his father, who was an actor and a bon vivant. When Sacha was a little boy, he asked his nurse, at bedtime, where his father was going. In his autobiography he says:

> She answered, "He's going to work, and earn some money for you." Seeing my astonishment she added, "Well, he's going to play this evening."
> I fell asleep with the idea that a man could earn money by playing; and I grew up with the idea that "play" was a synonym for the word "work." I haven't changed my idea.

The same experience can be felt differently by different people. When my daughters were very small, we lived in many places. Today, one loves travel and moves easily from apartment to apartment. The other craves roots, owns a home, and enjoys her "place."

Among other early experiences, "first times" are strong impressions, as are special events. Did you attend a funeral, a wake, see a dead person? What did you imagine death to be like? Birth? How did you think babies were born? Did you ever watch a pet giving birth? How were you disciplined? Ever spanked? Do you recall trips or holidays that were especially exciting? Disappointing? Did you have a really scary moment? Where did you sleep? What kind of bed? With someone or alone? Wet your bed?

What kind of food do you remember? What were the dishes and table setting like? Who combed your hair? When was the first time you wore lipstick? High heels? Was there one high point in your earliest years that comes to mind quickly?

EDUCATION

Childhood years of learning differ from adult education. When we are children education is mostly foisted on us, and we often have to suffer through it.

An abundance of material shows a dislike-to-hatred of school and teachers, especially among later achievers. There are exceptions, but ordinary, regimented schooling usually imposes a mass suppression of creativity, spontaneity, and individuality.

In a study of 400 eminent people, researchers found that three out of five intensely disliked their schools, especially the teachers. They were often bullied by their schoolmates and misunderstood by their teachers.

A leading professor of education said: "Society is downright savage in its treatment of creative people, particularly when they are young."

Albert Einstein was thought dull and even backward by his teachers, who reported to his father that he was mentally slow, unsociable, and adrift forever in his foolish dreams. Paul Cézanne was rejected by the Beaux Arts School, and Emile Zola got a zero in literature.

Sacha Guitry especially hated his headmaster:

At this moment I write as the man remembering, not as the child speaking ... and I remember perfectly ... I can see him now ... idiotic gravity ... for what reason? To terrify a child of seven? Why should all lycées give off the atmosphere of prisons?

When school and teachers are good, education can be the best part of life. One youngster was told by a teacher that "it was a pleasure to teach an intelligent little girl who wished to learn." This compliment elicited the response: "I am sure that one sentence settled my destiny for life."

Most of you can remember similar scenes that shaped your lives. Gather these threads and see how they are drawn through life. Do you recall your first day of school? Did you get into trouble? Did you have one special friend? What was your favorite subject or teacher? The least favorite?

BODY CONTACT

Scientists have discovered that babies who are not fondled can get sick—even die—from an actual illness they call "skin hunger." Good touching is essential to development, self-esteem, relationships with people.

Negative touch can have negative effects. One student lived in dread fear that when a particular uncle visited, she would be obliged to accept his wet kiss on her mouth.

Touching is a way of relating, the lack of it a way of distancing. It also develops the sense of body freedom and the ability to play and have fun.

Dena Davida, a dancer in Montreal, teaches a modern experimental dance technique called Contact Improvisation. In one exercise, she asks students to recall early sensations of touching. Children have no trouble doing this. Here are some Kid Contacts:

At age eight, asking my grandmother to sit on my back. She did it to please me, and I felt especially close to her then.

Weaving in and out of my father's legs. I felt a sense of his protection and play combined. What a sweet feeling!

Blankets over heads, lights off, we touched hands and bodies, rolling anonymously. It was definitely sensual, and abandoned.

My sister would stiffen and bridge over two beds; I'd crawl over her back, watch out for alligators below. Scary and exciting. Looking back, I was probably not aware that there was a new thrill in discovering how many things could be done with my body.

SEX

Fortunately, science now labels all the early sexual experiences as normal: masturbation, playing with one another's bodies with curiosity. Babies get gratification any way they can and have sexual feelings from birth.

The trouble begins when society imposes mores, usually along with adolescence and puberty—the worst time it could choose. Just when preteens get scared and excited by their feelings and the awakening of romantic love, the boom is lowered on its full expression.

Your sex life in youth will include some of the following issues, the result of natural development and social conflicts:

Your earliest memories of physical sexual feelings.

Early experiments with self and others.

How you got sex information and misinformation.

Social censorship through parents, teachers, church, others.

Conflicts such as that between the need for variety in sex experiences and the need for a stable relationship.

Childhood sex fantasies as to what sex looked like, how conception worked, and so on.

When children are restricted and not educated about sex, they fantasize in sometimes sad, amusing, but always imaginative ways.

One of the most common assumptions made by children is that babies come from kissing—largely a result of watching old movies that did not show the rest of the action as many films do now. Actress Anne Jackson, in her autobiography, says, "Kids had such misconceptions. You could get pregnant from a *terlit* if a man went ahead of you—even if it was your brother."

One student had fantasized sex as two distinctly different acts, one bad (done by unmarried people in the nude) and the other O.K. (by married couples, probably wearing clothes).

Your story need not sound inhibited about sex. This is one area in particular to keep free and warm. More needs to be written about the details of these young experiences, explicit in the mechanics of sex play, but not written mechanically. Elaborate on the feelings and effects on your life as a result. You can add information to the science bank and help other readers remove any stigma about things *they* did as a child. Your experience can dispel guilt feelings about secret sex capers when readers know they were not alone in this activity. And it adds color to your story. It will not come across as pornography if your motives are honest and integrated with the style and theme.

FANTASIES

Our culture tends to suppress fantasies. Children with vivid fantasies are often thought peculiar or mentally disturbed. Many psychology books still in circulation connect fantasizing (or "daydreaming") with autistic or schizophrenic tendencies. They say the child is controlled by inner desires and not by outer reality. Studies were done to classify the types of fantasies into "conquering hero," "suffering hero," or "rehearsal for life." The conquering-hero type is considered healthier than the suffering one because to conquer is to be aggressive, to overcome odds, to destroy opposition, and to attain status and recognition. Attitudes toward fantasy are strongly tied to social stereotypes and expectations.

But autobiographies of achievers are generously laced with examples of childhood fantasies. Many continued this behavior through adulthood, especially those who were encouraged to set their imaginations free and their creativity to blossom.

Isaac Bashevis Singer, who was awarded the 1978 Nobel Prize for Literature, said:

> I'm a daydreamer. I was a daydreamer when I was a child and, in this respect, I haven't aged at all . . . some of my stories grow out of the daydreaming . . . literature is actually a form of daydreaming.

Albert Einstein invented his own religion and chanted hymns to a deity of his own creation. Eleanor Roosevelt fantasized herself as the mistress of her dead father's household.

When Anatole France was barely four, he watched a man repair the wallpaper. Underneath was more wallpaper, and behind that, small dark holes. Peering into the holes, France believed he saw creatures and heard their sounds. They were misshapen beings, busying themselves with musical instruments, saucepans, and saws. They were with him for years. Later, he fantasized entire plays come to life with his fingers, ribbons, and crayons—playing various parts, being costumed.

Gertrude Stein had a secret world with its own language. The Tolstoy children had a secret society of Moravian brothers who were creating a perfect world.

Imaginary companions are common to about a third of children between the ages of two and a half and four and a half. To the children they are quite real, with names and stable characters. When they depart, it is often with dramatic flourish such as a horrible accident, or being killed in an Indian war. They generally disappear when the child enters school.

So if you ever had an imaginary playmate, haul him (or her or it) out and tell about it. You're in fine company.

FRIENDS, PLAY, AND TOYS

Friendship in youth is normally intense. You may have had one special, special friend. Or a string of special friends. You probably ran with a rat pack if you were let out in the neighborhood. If not, don't worry, many gifted children were withdrawn from schoolmates and neighborhood children.

Think carefully about the role you played, most of the time. Were you a leader or a follower? Passive or aggressive? Innovative or tradition bound?

Isadora Duncan wrote:

> When I was about six years old, my mother came home one day and found that I had collected half a dozen babies from the neighborhood—all too young to walk—and had them sitting before me on the floor while I was teaching them to wave their arms. When she asked the explanation of this, I informed her that it was my school of the dance.

Many mothers would have become hysterical, rushed to return the babies, and disciplined the six-year-old. Isadora was luckier than most. Her mother was amused and sat down at the piano to play for them. Isadora later developed her famous school of dance.

Toys would be highly personal if left to the choice of the children. But these days of merchandising, toys often teach children how to prepare for the future in insidious ways. The fashion doll that needs trunks of clothes, fully accessorized, has replaced the baby doll and rag doll, who just needed lots of loving.

Children are trained to demand everything they see on television. Did you? Did you have the usual modern child's toy-stuffed room, or did you make your own toys? Were your toys sex-role stereotyped—that is, dolls for girls and woodworking for boys? Did you have a grandparent who made old-fashioned toys for you? Mostly, how did you feel about your toys? Which was a favorite—and why?

FOOD

Mom's kitchen is an emotionally charged place, and is connected with intimacy. Many autobiographies are written around food, and recipe books can be memory trips. A charming one is *Reminiscence and Ravioli*, Nika Standen's recipe book based on her memorable summers spent with an aunt and uncle in a small Italian town.

PETS

They can be extremely important, and real family members. When an allergist tried to remove our family cat, my daughter cried bitterly through her sneezes, "We can't give Pesita away, Mommy, she's my *sister!*" Doris Lessing wrote a cat autobiography, *Particularly Cats*, about the succession of cats through her family life and their individual personalities.

HOLIDAYS

Often these are high points in a child's memory. Sometimes they set the scene for later preferences such as nostalgia for the sea, the desert, or the mountains.

RELIGION

How did it shape your later philosophical sway? Did you renounce or embrace a faith?

Sense impression is the important ingredient in these early memories. Think of all five senses: sight, sound, touch, smell, and taste. Narrow them down: the smell of lilacs, the taste of a wild strawberry, the softness of grandmother's bosom. These conjure up memories of entire summers, a particular relationship, or a turning point. Marcel Proust's *Remembrance of Things Past* was triggered by the smell of a *madeleine*.

Among aspiring autobiographers there are always a few who have gotten as far as "I was born in the year XXXX, in the town of XYZ. My parents were XX and XY. My earliest memory was getting stuck with a needle and screaming. I was told later that happened at the pediatrician's office when I was three and a half." At this point, there is a great deal of staring at the typewriter. Then what? Now that I'm born, what do I do?

Don't panic. There are myths to be exorcized around the "proper" way to begin an autobiography. Most people think they have to begin at the beginning. That isn't so. You don't have to reconstruct a chronological and orderly record of your life before you can start writing. In fact, a chronological autobiography is probably the dullest way to begin. The "I was born" story opening usually causes the reader to riffle through the beginning to get to the interesting parts, if inspired to riffle at all.

Here's how Sacha Guitry solved his beginning:

> I was born on February 21, 1885. There is nothing in this revelation to move the reader to tears, I concede, but it must be agreed that for me this is a date.

Writing technique calls for a *hook* at the beginning, something catchy to hold the reader's interest, and a chain of hooks to keep him interested.

If your childhood was not interesting enough to you to build the beginning of your story on, go directly to what you believe was the most memorable time of your life. Begin there—if no better idea comes to mind. You can return later to the earlier periods or refer to them intermittently as you need to. Many autobiographers dispense altogether with their youth.

First memories are usually momentary and not always significant. Many notable people had late or weak memories, among them Rousseau, Bunyan, Darwin, and Trollope.

A researcher said:

> There would appear to be as many remembering at two years as after four years. Casanova recalls nothing before eight years and four months, which is unusually late as his sexual experiences were early, for they began at ten years old.

Few Westerners claim self-awareness during the first years, but it is commonly reported in Eastern and metaphysical literature. The Yogi Yogananda's autobiography says:

> I find my earliest memories covering the anachronistic features of the previous incarnation. Clear recollections came to me of a distant life in which I had been a yogi amid Himalayan snows. These glimpses of the past, by some dimensionless link, also afforded me a glimpse of the future.

He then describes helpless feelings of his body's "impotence," and resentment and humiliation at not being able to walk.

We mortals have to rely on "as told to" accounts of our birth and infancy. Most autobiographers refer to one or two dim memories before the age of three or four.

If you are a young adult, you will be tempted to exaggerate, having comparatively less life experience. Stick close to universal experiences, for example, the early dawn of selfhood—the moment when you knew you were *you*. This has been an all-time favorite "wonder-of-it-all" experience.

Roger North, born in the mid-seventeenth century, told of the first day in school: "I began to have a sense of myself." One hundred and fifty years later, upon the close of an early consciousness-raising group for men, one member wrote in a collective autobiographical story of the group experience of "being eleven years old and grooving on summer, my bike, swimming, no shirt, insects, and the discovery that I am a person. A caterpillar is a caterpillar and I'm me!"

Psychologists have made it fashionable to segment our lives into stages of development, "periods of life which differ in function and relative emphasis from other periods." We become ready, by stages, to walk, think in abstract terms, and add skills, and we do this within a wide range of individual differences. No stage is better or more mature than another. Each has its purpose. Each is necessary, natural. Theoretical embellishment is often given this subject. Some authorities would have us believe that we must go through this or that at a certain age. We are doomed to lifelong neuroses if we did not "properly" pass from one stage to another—at the "appropriate" age level.

But if you start looking at your life like that, it can cause you anything from minor discomforts to major anxieties. You may begin to regard your growth too clinically and see it tied up in little bundles of time patterns and age groups. You can be made to feel retarded, deviant, or weird if your childhood patterns did not conform to some established parameter of psychosexual stages (à la Freud), developmental personality stages (à la Erikson), or cognitive stages (à la Piaget).

There's another way of looking at your life. Transitions are lifelong events. Something new happens every day, starting from the first time you crossed the street alone, rode your first bike, saw your first bluebird.

But since you are exposed to powerful pressures to adapt, adjust, conform, and compete on certain manufactured standardized levels, you'll find similarities between your natural, uncontaminated mode of development and that expected of you.

An interesting adjunct to the study of your personality development is to run through a few standard lists and see how they apply to you. The lists will be useful if you, your therapist, or your parents were inclined toward the Freudian approach. Even if they weren't, these concepts probably influenced you somewhere along the way.

Freud recognized five psychosexual stages:

1. *Oral.* Up to two years. Sucking predominates—sense of being at one with the mother. Orthodox Freudians believe that if we were not nursed properly, we are in trouble.

2. *Anal.* Up to three years. A power play between child and parent for control, centered around toilet training.

3. *Phallic.* Up to six. Energy focused on genitals. The Oedipal complex develops: the son is attached to the mother. To develop normally, he must transfer to an identity with the father.

4. *Latency.* Heterosexuality is repressed. Preteens don't like the opposite sex.

5. *Genital.* Adolescence. Heterosexuality reappears.

Erik Erikson became very popular in the fifties and sixties as the result of the publication of his books *Childhood and Society* and *Identity, Youth and Crisis.* He brought to public attention the concept of life cycles and the "identity crisis."
In brief, his stages are:

1. *Trust.* Without proper mothering, attention, and love the child acquires *distrust,* becomes sickly and neurotic.

2. *Autonomy.* The toddler must learn to "walk on his own two feet." *Dependency* is a consequence of improper teaching.

3. *Initiative.* The preschooler should be allowed to explore and to move into specific behaviors involving planning and purpose. If not, the result is *guilt* and its accompanying neuroses.

4. *Industry.* The schoolchild learns to be a worker and acquires skills. Otherwise, *inferiority* is the consequence.

5. *Identity.* The adolescent. The task at this stage is personal and sexual identification. The opposite: *role confusion.*

6. *Intimacy* versus *isolation.*

7. *Generation* versus *stagnation.*

8. *Ego integrity* versus *despair*

The last three are the adult stages.

Since Erikson, cycle theories and therapies have mushroomed on the psychological scene, with followers becoming trendy or confused.

But I caution you again: don't get too clinical with yourself. Rather, focus on yourself as an individual. Comparing yourself with others or measuring yourself against theories dilutes and distorts your identity. Society manipulates us enough without our helping it along.

If you were not raised according to someone's book, you don't have to consider yourself a freak or a victim of an irreversible disease. Keep a vigil on a balanced life.

Researchers V. and M. G. Goertzel presented three case histories to groups of graduate students in education. They were asked to predict what the following children would be like in five years: average-normal; psychotic; neurotic; delinquent; or mentally deficient. (Make a note of your answers.)

Case 1: Girl, sixteen, orphaned, willed to custody of grandmother by mother. . . . Mother rejected the homely child. . . . Grandmother . . . dresses her oddly, refuses to let her have playmates. . . .

Case 2: Boy, sent home from school . . . because of nervous breakdown. Poor student, no friends. . . . Spoke late . . . odd mannerisms . . . chants hymns to himself.

Case 3: Boy . . . large head at birth, thought to have brain fever. . . . Relatives and neighbors think he is abnormal. . . . considered mentally ill by teacher.

The Goertzels comment:

> When Eleanor Roosevelt, Albert Einstein, and Thomas Edison had been categorized by our audience as delinquent, mentally ill, and retarded, respectively, we spoke of the danger of making snap decisions on superficial, incomplete evidence.

So beware of snap judgments about yourself. As an autobiographer you may be leading your five-year-old self around by the hand, making decisions about how he or she felt back then, through your adult senses.

When we were young, we saw things as a child. Spitteler said: "There is no consciousness of being a child. The child is a poetic invention of adults."

EXERCISE 1. BABY BOOK _____

PURPOSE OF THIS EXERCISE

You may often remember past events through your present perspective or mood. If you are in a depression, the past can seem more negative than it really was. You may even tack things onto past events that didn't exist. This exercise will help bridge that gap.

INSTRUCTIONS

1. Use a large photograph album, about 12 × 14 inches.

2. Starting with your first photograph, paste in significant pictures of your choice, according to the Wheel of Life diagram in Chapter 1, using one or two pages for each section.

3. Study each section of photos for emotional content: Did you seem happy or unhappy? Disturbed or relaxed? In tune with the other person or group, or detached?

4. Write a sentence or paragraph about each section.

EXAMPLE (A DIVORCÉE):

1. Up to 7 years — I notice for the first time that I smile in most photos, but without opening my mouth. I seem content, but there is no sense of joy. I am next to people, but not close to any.

2. 8 to 14 years — I'm beginning to put my arms around people, reluctantly with adults, more comfortably with peers. I still don't hold my head up, but look upward as a child, scared. I'm warmest with my cat.

3. 15 to 21 years — I seem happiest when I'm with girl friends, shy with boys. I'm standing straighter, but still no sense of joy.

4. 22 to 28 years — I'm withdrawn again. Much inner activity suggests contemplation and confusion. This is during marriage. The smiles are phony.

5. 29 to 35 years — Alone with my children, I seem happy for the first time. I'm still not standing straight. Still looking up, meekly.

6. 36 to 42 years — Photographs at my job in the office look the most put-together ever! I show a different kind of happiness. I'm standing straight and looking directly at everyone!

7. 43 to 50 years — I look like a grown-up at last. The smiles are sincere. Hey! I'm showing my teeth when I smile!

EXERCISE 2. THE ORIGINAL CHILD _____

PURPOSE OF THIS EXERCISE

    To project yourself back into time when you were a child, with that child's point of view. To learn how to communicate freely with that child.

INSTRUCTIONS

  1. Browse through your Baby Book, and stop when you get to a picture that seems to want to tell you something.

  2. Study the picture in a relaxed, meditative way, allowing your subconscious to take over as best you can. (If you can do this with self-hypnosis, so much the better.)

  3. Using the child's scrawl of its period, and becoming that child, write a paragraph, addressing your present adult, telling what's on your mind and how you feel.

I love my daddy, mommy makes him take bak the cote he bot me, I feel sad

EXERCISE 3. DIALOGUE: ADULT TO CHILD _____

PURPOSE OF THIS EXERCISE
    To reach back to a situation in childhood that caused a scar, and begin the process of healing wounds of the past that may still exist as irritants or pain.

INSTRUCTIONS
1. Study the photograph and child's writing in Exercise 2 for a moment.
2. Call forth your best adult wisdom. Write a paragraph, addressing the child in the photograph. Explain why the incident occurred from the point of view of the person or persons involved. Tell how everyone else felt. Offer the child alternative feelings and behavior. Tell the child what he or she needed to hear then.

EXAMPLE (SAME PERSON AS IN EXERCISE 2):
    You look very pretty in that coat, but it's the wrong size. Daddy should have bought a bigger size. He couldn't refuse you when you fell in love with it. You could have listened to what Mommy said to him—that if he had bought a larger size, she could have taken it in and you could have worn it longer. That money was a problem. And that buying you things was not a sign that he loved you more than Mommy did. They both loved you. Mommy worked day and night for you. There will be lots of coats.

READINGS

ADAMS, HENRY. *The Education of Henry Adams.* New York: Random House, 1931. Henry Adams felt there were burdens imposed on the privileged child, and he wrote about his early years in the third person to "distance" himself from the historical pressures on him.

BATES, E. STUART. *Inside Out: An Introduction to Autobiography.* See Readings, Chapter 1, for notes.

BERGER, JOSEF, and BERGER, DOROTHY. *Small Voices.* New York: Paul S. Eriksson, 1966. As enchanting, free, colorful, and honest as children's paintings, this is "a grown-up's treasury of selections from the diaries, journals, and notebooks of small children." Don't miss it.

BRADLEY, MIKE; DANCHIK, LONNIE; FAGER, MARTY; and WODETSKI, TOM. *Unbecoming Men.* New York: Times Change Press, 1971. Written by four men from one of the first men's consciousness-raising groups about their experience in discovering societal pressures on men that warp their personalities and stunt their growth.

DAVIDA, DENA. "Kid Contact." *Contact Magazine.* Stinson Beach, Calif., summer 1977. A charming article in this beautifully executed and highly informational periodical relating to people's experiences with, and understanding of, their bodies.

DUNCAN, ISADORA. *My Life.* New York: Boni and Liveright, 1972. A most readable story that exemplifies Isadora's sense of freedom and how her early conditioning promoted it. Her work and her love life are coordinated and understandable within her own philosophy.

ERIKSON, ERIK H. *Identity, Youth and Crisis.* New York: W. W. Norton & Co., 1968. A psychiatric approach to childhood and the adolescent years.

GOERTZEL, V., and GOERTZEL, M.G. *Cradles of Eminence.* Boston: Little, Brown & Co., 1962. An extraordinary study of the backgrounds of 400 eminent people, with unexpected findings as to what factors led to their achievement.

GUITRY, SACHA. *If Memory Serves.* Garden City, N.Y.: Doubleday, Doran, 1935. One of the most charming stories of a life with a positive view. An insight into the soul of a Frenchman with true joi de vivre.

MUIR, EDWIN. *An Autobiography.* London: The Hogarth Press, 1954. A poet and naturalist wrote this beautiful book with profound insights into the process of inviting memories and the relationship between the child and the later adult.

NIN, ANAÏS. *Linotte: The Early Diary of Anaïs Nin, 1914–1920.* New York: Harcourt Brace Jovanovich, 1979. Nin's early work has richness of expression and self-insight unusual in a young girl.

SPITTELER, CARL. *Autobiography.* Jena: Firma Diederichs, 1914. A magnificent accomplishment in the restoring of memories of the first four years, with commentaries by the adult about his childhood feelings.

STANDEN, NIKA. *Reminiscence and Ravioli.* New York: William Morrow & Co., 1946. Half recipe book and half autobiography of Mrs. Standen's early childhood when she spent several months of each year with a lively aunt and uncle. A vivid picture of a small Italian town, bursting with anecdotes, characters, and descriptions of eating habits.

THOMAS, R. MURRAY. *Comparing Theories of Child Development.* Belmont, Calif.: Wadsworth Publishing Co., 1979. Studious account of this field of research that helps sort out "facts" as we know them thus far.

TOURNIER, PAUL. *A Place for You.* New York: Harper & Row, 1968. A lovely and poetic survey of the subject of one's "place" by a leading philosopher and writer.

YOGANANDA, PARAMAHANSA. *The Autobiography of a Yogi.* Los Angeles: Self-Realization Fellowship, 1959. An extraordinary, highly readable life account. Covers a broad span of years, travel, and personality development. Self-understanding, the goal, is thoroughly explained as he accomplished it.

4

Adulthood

*Everyone has his own specific
vocation or mission in life:
everyone must carry out a concrete
assignment that demands fulfillment.
Therein he cannot be
replaced, nor his life repeated.
Thus, everyone's task is as
unique as his special opportunity
to implement it.*

—VIKTOR FRANKEL

When does adulthood begin? Most people, after a few moments' thought, can point to a moment in their lives when they suddenly felt grown-up. As you become more acquainted with the details of your own development, you will realize that you grew up in more than one moment—bit by bit sometimes and by leaps and bounds at other times. Thanatologists, the psychologists who study death and dying, tell us that we don't die all at once, either. We die many little deaths.

As children we grow out in many directions; later we narrow things down. As we get older we get focused and make selections. We learn we can't do everything or be everything or have everything. We choose vocations, avocations, mates, life-styles, beliefs, biases. We decide what is important to us. Youth looks ahead, but adults, sooner or later, look back. In reviewing your life for your autobiography, what matters most is your attitude.

All of life is educational and what you have learned through your experiences will be educational for your readers.

Self-authority is a sign of adult thinking. Of course we need one another, but for adult reasons: to share ideas, feelings, and activities. But as adults we rely less and less on others and more on ourselves for the decisions and design of our lives. Writing an autobiography is a perfect way to make a comprehensive inventory of our priorities in life.

A wise man once told me, "You must stop for a moment before you do whatever you think is important and ask yourself, 'What is important?' " Those three words were for me like the sounding of a gong. I took time out for a moral inventory: Who says *this* is important? My conscience? My peers? Parents? Fear of the eyes of the world upon me? God?

As you review your life, review your shifting priorities. Are they the same or different from a year ago, five years ago? What are the most important things to you now?

Gandhi wrote in his autobiography:

> What I want to achieve, what I have been striving and pining to achieve these thirty years, is self-realization, to see God face to face. . . . All that I do by way of speaking and writing, and all my ventures in the political field, are directed to this same end.

Those who have an all-encompassing, sharply defined goal early in life are lucky. But it need not be Gandhi's ultimate, lifetime type of goal.

While a single focused goal is important to achievement, there is a danger. One can also become lopsided, and neglect the other aspects of one's life.

Give some hard thought to where most of your energy goes. Is one goal dominant? Are there many goals? Too many? Diffused goals? Have you neglected an area of interest? Are you continually saying, "Some day I'll have time for *that?*"

It doesn't matter what is important to you in terms of universal values. This is not a moral issue. It's entirely personal and not a question of inferior versus superior goals. It's merely a question of where you have been and where you are now. It's information for your project. Don't make any judgment.

If having fun and taking each day as it comes is your major life's interest, what's wrong with that? Enjoying life is surely a major goal. If your life revolves around your work, marriage, children, or public service, that's part of your story. Your value system or what is important to you is the foundation of your autobiography.

When you've decided what is important, components of your life begin to regroup. Certain things join the "important" group and are awarded more energy; other things are minimized or eliminated.

You may find that when you gain insight and become ready to take on new aspects of living, there is often a period of euphoria, a sense of relief, release, and freedom—followed by a sudden and mysterious depression. Sometimes this is called "the mourning period" for what you gave up, whether material, ideas, people, or "games" they've played. People resist change.

In life there are things we can't have, simply because in life we can't have it all. As children we gobble up all experiences. Adults must settle for less. We make peace with the fact that when we walk into a library or bookstore we will not be able to read *all* those books. If we're crazy about sex, we can't possess *all* the people who turn us on. Why, then, do some dwell on things they've missed or thought they've missed?

There is an innate striving toward perfection, completeness, wholeness. But wholeness doesn't mean having everything— just what belongs to us. This can be achieved with quality, not quantity.

You can develop a positive view of what seems negative or deficient in your life story. You may be a woman without a career. Your time and energy went into homemaking and motherhood. That's your story, and an important one. It was a choice you needed to make at that time. Many kinds of experiences have two sides.

Lost opportunities were lost because we had impulses or needs for other things, valid in their time and place.

Mistakes can be seen as stepping-stones.

Accidents can set us back, but they add experience as well as empathy for others who shared the experience.

People lost to us by death or desertion gave us emotional and psychological knowledge and depth

Crises called on reserves we sometimes didn't know were there.

Something missing may be a part of your body. It may be a relative who is ill.

The most inspiring life stories are those of people who learned that it's not what they have but what they do with it that counts.

It often slips our minds to do the simplest and most therapeutic thing available—at all times and with no cost: count our blessings.

Somerset Maugham, in *The Summing Up*, his personal search for truth and goodness, concludes:

> It seems that I have little more to say than can be read in any copybook or heard from any pulpit. . . . What is right action? . . . The best answer I know is that given by Fray Luis de Leon. . . . The beauty of life, he says, is nothing but this, that each should act in conformity with his nature and his business.

Cycles or stages of life are evident in adulthood as well as in childhood, but they are *your* stages, not those delineated by authority. There are stages of growth on all levels designed by nature: physical, psychological, mental, and emotional.

Stages designed by psychologists and sociologists may be interesting and provocative, and truly helpful to some at some times, but they can also be speculative, conflicting, and confusing. Dag Hammarskjöld had his *Markings* or signposts, Gail Sheehy speaks of *Passages*, Phil Donahue refers to his *phases*. It's important to keep an open mind about how your life was "supposed to" develop. If you review it in terms of your personal partitions, you won't put limitations and judgments on yourself.

Theories can limit the human potential. Developmental psychology is an immature science. We still don't quite know what goes on in the minds of babies. There is no established field of infant psychology. New theories are constantly replacing old ones. Take "baby's first step" as an example: Textbooks tell us we start to walk at about thirteen months. But a group of scientists gathered evidence of musculature ability of babies to walk at two weeks!

In theories of aging and longevity, the average life span is about seventy. But Shirali Mislimov, in southwestern Russia, is said to have lived 168 years. Li Chung Yun, a Chinese herbalist, died in 1933 allegedly at the age of 256, with his twenty-fourth wife at his side. For you skeptics: Dr. L. Sukharebsky, director of the Public Institute of Juvenology in Moscow, has said, "Scientists believe that the human being can live not just one hundred years, but four hundred years or even more." Fundamentalists, those who take the Bible literally, point to the long lives of biblical characters.

However, we more often receive the message such as one from a researcher at a university school of gerontology who told a group of "seniors" (age fifty and over) to "compensate" for the "natural loss of physical and sexual abilities" at their age!

Theories can have a doomsday effect, becoming self-fulfilling prophesies. So beware of taking too literally any theories, including mine. The danger is being seduced into judging yourself harshly if you don't meet its standards of normality. It's all hypothetical, anyway.

It's safer to check out who was studied, in what era, under what conditions, and who is doing the studying. For example, Else Frenkel-Brunswick, the first cycle psychologist, theorized that "people" go through five definite phases. The study was of 400 persons, including Queen Victoria, John D. Rockefeller, and Casanova. Hardly representative of the rest of us.

By now, you probably have a clearer idea of how your unique combination of events group themselves into personal periods and of your own categories—what was important to you.

If you are a young adult, your experiences may be explored primarily as preparation for the future. If you are an older person, you may be haunted by paths not trodden, musty mistakes, goals not accomplished. Retrieve, as well, your memory's treasure trove of experiences you did have. Reliving can be as sweet the second time around. Concentrate on how much you know and how much you have to give the younger generation. Leaving something of yourself behind, especially ideas, is a form of immortality.

As adults, we integrate our categories. Love, sex, work, play, marriage, parenthood, and our place and tasks in the community blend into what we call the well-rounded or balanced life.

Life skills become a smooth and harmonious operation most of us hope to accomplish. Few do.

But your story is one of striving toward completeness. You're not through yet. Remember, the autobiography is an unfinished story. When you look at it clearly so far, you can plot your future more clearly.

Your story—to be continued—is another future autobiography.

EXERCISE 1. GIANT STEPS

PURPOSE OF THIS EXERCISE

To practice a positive point of view about your past adult life, bringing back memories of the good things that happened.

Do this honestly and thoroughly to avoid a "poor me" note sneaking into your autobiography—if such is your inclination.

INSTRUCTIONS

Using the Wheel of Life diagram in Chapter 1, list the one or two major positive events or inner experiences you had in each section of your *adult years*.

EXAMPLE (A THIRTY-FIVE-YEAR-OLD MALE SCHOOLTEACHER):

Section 4—Ages 16–25—Years 1962–1966. Summers in the country. Learned to communicate with animals. Learned to swim, ride, hike. My first mad crush—on Zelda.

Section 5—Ages 21–25—Years 1967–1971. My first real job. Discovered that I can make money selling real estate. The power of independence.

Section 6—Ages 26–30—Years 1972–1976. Running into Harvey and getting turned on to college. Put myself through college.

Section 7—Ages 31–35—Years 1977–1981. Floundering with courses. Lousy teachers led me to decision to teach. Getting robbed by high school gang—led to decision to teach high school.

EXERCISE 2. COUNT YOUR BLESSINGS _____

PURPOSE OF THIS EXERCISE

To take an inventory of the good things you have now. As you write your story, tie these in with events that led up to your present positives.

INSTRUCTIONS

List the material, vocational, and social positive categories in your life acquired through adult years.

EXAMPLE (WOMAN WRITER IN HER FIFTIES):

Money—Financial security. (A long hard pull to get to this point.)

Love, sex—Extremely satisfying. (Many major problems to get here, but all is stable and serene most of the time.)

Friends—I now have as many as I want and need. (Years of loneliness and being used by people taught me to appreciate my present friends and to be cautious and selective from now on.)

Work—The ultimate is mine: to make money doing what I love the most—writing. And I can create my own projects. (I remember what it was like to hate my jobs.)

Family—I have a small family, but a warm and satisfying life with them. (Therapy helped me work out problems with parents, husband, and child. Now I'm looking forward to grandmotherhood.)

EXERCISE 3. MORAL INVENTORY _____

PURPOSE OF THIS EXERCISE

As you develop your story, you may want to keep an eye on your personality and character development.

INSTRUCTIONS

Make a list of your positive personality traits and their opposites. I call the latter "challenges."
Score yourself on a scale from 0 to 100.

Positive Traits	Challenges
Self-esteem	Self-pity
Humility	Arrogance
Honesty, self-honesty	Dishonesty, guile
Patience	Impatience
Love	Hate, resentments
Forgiveness	Unforgiving, hold grudges
Trust	Distrust
Independence	Dependence
Generosity	Stingy, holding back
Productivity	Not living up to potential
Promptness	Procrastination
Straightforwardness	Insincerity
Self-appreciation	Jealousy
Positive thinking	Negative thinking
Look for the good	Critical

READINGS

DONAHUE, PHIL. *Donahue, My Own Story*. New York: Simon & Schuster, 1979. Like his television show, and mostly about the background of the show, this excellent book deals with issues important to him, and his phases in achieving understanding.

ERIKSON, ERIK. *Identity, Youth and Crisis*. See Readings, Chapter 3, for notes.

FRANKEL, VIKTOR E. *Man's Search for Meaning*. New York: Simon & Schuster, 1971. Frankel's story of his physical, psychological, and spiritual survival from a Nazi concentration camp.

GANDHI, MOHANDAS K. *An Autobiography*. Boston: Beacon Press, 1957. Gandhi writes in great detail his mission—to achieve union with God—and how everything was thrown into this struggle after he made the decision.

GOODMAN, ELLEN. *Turning Points*. New York: Doubleday & Co. 1979. We are caught in a "shuttle zone" between our need to change and established value systems. We need security and roots, but we also need to take risks and explore the new.

GUITRY, SACHA. *If Memory Serves.* See Readings, Chapter 2, for notes.

HERRIOT, JAMES. *All Things Bright and Beautiful.* New York: Bantam Books, 1973. A popular and charming account of life as a veterinary surgeon in the Yorkshire Dales. His story is about "the ordinary things which have always made up our lives."

MAUGHAM, W. SOMERSET. *The Summing Up.* Garden City, N. Y.: Doubleday & Co., 1953. Maugham's philosophy about people, society, and mostly writing. He reveals as much as he knows about himself and is disarmingly honest.

SHEEHY, GAIL. *Passages: Predictable Crises of Adult Life.* New York: E. P. Dutton, 1974. A study of 115 cases of middle-class adults from eighteen to fifty years. Popular, but theories are controversial.

5

Pruning Your Roots

*The man who has not anything to boast
of but his illustrious ancestors is like
a potato—the only good belonging to
him is underground.*

—SIR THOMAS OVERBURY, 1614

Alex Haley called the pursuit of his roots a twelve-year obsession. Louis Kirkjian, during two years of self-confessed "temporary insanity," created a mural-sized family tree chart showing 1,777 of his Armenian relatives. It's easy to get hooked on family-history data collecting, even to develop "rootamania."

Unless you are planning a family record only, stick to your story, and pull the family around as needed to develop it. Collect enough relevant data. If new material appears that changes your idea or inspires a new one, use it, providing you honestly feel it's better than the original.

You may be drowning in material, but if you have a sparse and inadequate amount, there are four basic useful steps in collecting and harvesting historical data:

1. Gather everything you have at hand. This means going through trunks, files, basements, and attics for all past documents, letters, old diaries, photographs, home movies, tape recordings, clothing, tax records, and miscellaneous mementos. You may face the horror of cleaning out stuffed and musty closets; you may already have your

70

things neatly stored; or you may be the type who knows where to lay your hands on every piece of paper.

2. Do the same type of collecting from available friends and relatives, even doctors and former business associates. Memories of your oldest living relatives are invaluable. Haley started by listening to the older women in his family give back-porch reminiscences. Visit everyone you can, or invite them over in groups or en masse for a "roots" party. Forewarn them, though, and ask them to bring along material to share. Tape-record and take notes of as much of the session as you can, encouraging reminiscing along the lines you are interested in. These sessions can produce everything from mild disagreements to roaring fights over who did what and when, whether important or trivial. At one of my family gatherings there was a heated argument about which way our grandmother folded her blintzes!

3. Telephone or write out-of-towners. First send a query-type letter to feel them out. Find out how much cooperation you can expect. If they are cooperative, be ready to follow up with a more comprehensive questionnaire, or a series. Ask how their memories touch your life—what they thought of you then, what you looked like to them, what you wore, liked to eat, mannerisms, anecdotes. Scraps of information often get put together at the finish line in a patterned design. If their memories don't always fit with others', it's all the more interesting to know of varied personal impressions.

On the other hand, it's important to record somewhere as much of the truth as you know, even if you don't use it in writing your initial story. Let future descendants decide what is important to them. Your deletions are personal biases.

4. The family historian seeking complete information has a vast area in which to pursue his or her genealogy. The difference between a family history and a genealogy is that the latter requires legal documentation from public

records. The Southern California Genealogy Society (of the Sons of the Revolution) has as its motto: "There is no TRUTH without PROOF." It is most important to get correct names of relatives, with all the possible spellings used, and where they lived. Out of Paul Revere's autobiographical writings comes this example of the changes that can take place in a name far back in history:

It was DeRivoire, afterwards just Rivoire. Later, in America, my father changed it to Revere, so that, in his words, "the bumpkins could pronounce it!" But the Boston City records have spelt it as Reviere, Reveiere, Revear, and Reverie!

If you've gone as far as you can and still need more information, genealogy centers will provide you with a worldwide list of professional researchers. Data are useful only if they make a story point and are integrated into the story. One man got depressed when he discovered criminals among his noble ancestors. Then he discovered that the coat of arms he had claimed through his family name he wasn't entitled to use, since according to the rules, he was not a direct descendant of the original recipient. He suffered a loss of self-esteem until a researcher found a legitimate, different coat of arms for him, of a lesser but far more interesting group of swashbucklers. The man's personality changed. He became bolder, more outgoing. Through this experience, he realized that his own identity had various facets—but they were his, not his ancestors'. Now there's a story!

Another example is an adoptee who writes a question mark for "race" when she has to fill out forms. She is olive-skinned and doesn't know whether her origin is white, black, Indian, or Latin. In one of the many foster homes in which she was placed, the foster parents returned her to the orphanage because she was getting darker. At that point, she was told she was black. She lived as a black and married one. Later she was told she was white!

Your life has many stories, but there is usually a major theme. Keep this in mind as you collect data.

There are many kinds of facts. A fascinating approach was

worked out by Frank and Lillian Gilbreth, he an industrial engineer and she an industrial psychologist. They wanted to apply their planning skills to parenthood. They wanted twelve children, six boys and six girls. (They *had* six boys and six girls; later, two of the children wrote the best-seller, *Cheaper by the Dozen.*) When they were newlyweds they collected information about their combined families to know the kind of stock their children had to build on. Racial and experiential background does enter the picture in one way or another. But Lillian Gilbreth said, "Very little has been done in recording and studying the emotional lives of families, yet this material is most pertinent of all." She suggested looking for anecdotes, nicknames, how the family celebrated holidays, helped or hindered one another. These were seeds sown throughout the family histories that shaped their characters.

Add this information to the hard data of racial strains, national traditions and customs, and individual family traditions for a more interesting story.

Systems of data collecting are basically the same. Depending on the amount of material, you'll need anything from a simple looseleaf notebook to a filing cabinet. Pamphlet holders can be bought from a library supply house and fit neatly on bookshelves.

Categories your material with an index system. You can limit yourself to the seven periods of your life as discussed in the Wheel of Life exercise in Chapter 1. You can also use chronological life periods starting with elementary school, junior high, high school, college, graduate or trade school, marriage, parenthood, and retirement. If your life hasn't followed traditional lines, your categories might fit a social-change index system. If you have lived in different places, it can be one of locales or countries. If work is your major theme, your index can follow your career by positions held. One woman who had five husbands considered her life-styles and periods by that category.

Put your material in the best order you can for now. You can change it as you go. Do have some kind of system, or you'll find yourself in a tangle. But don't become overorganized at the expense of your writing output. If you can't find that special paper telling what year and month you moved into the dormitory, does it matter if it's a month or a year off?

There are special problems in some cases, vital to your story —let's say, if you're trying to track down a relative who may have had sickle-cell anemia. That would certainly affect you and your children. But if a problem can't be solved now, it's better left on the periphery of your story, if mentioned at all. Again, it all depends on whether it fits your major theme.

An example of a major theme is that of an adoptee who has not known a biological family. The Adoptees Liberty Movement Association (ALMA) helps people find their natural families, and Concerned United Birthparents (CUB) helps birthparents find their children. These and other organizations recognize the gnawing need for genetic identity. Others search beyond their parents for historical data, hoping to find a link to a renowned or royal ancestor. They will struggle for years trying to dig up even one VIP to identify with. Why?

One theory states that bloodlines make the person, claiming there is good, better, and best blood—and bad blood. Scientific data do not uphold this theory in relation to character, personality, or intelligence. There is much more evidence on the side of learned behavior. The problems of nature versus nurture, or heredity versus environment, is still unsolved and appears repeatedly in studies. We can inherit certain body structure, chemistry (whether due to climate, food, and other things), and genetic endowments, all of which, in certain mixtures, can result in personality tendencies. Body and mind are inseparable.

Lack of self-esteem drives some people to validate themselves through a prestigious ancestor, friend, lover, spouse, or idol. The main reason for writing your autobiography, however, is to validate yourself—to believe you are important, unique, and equivalent to anyone else. You have your own accomplishments.

Those who insist on pursuing pedigree as status are up against special problems of rulings. For example, one woman was anxious to be accepted into the Daughters of the American Revolution and searched fruitlessly for an ancestor—any old ancestor—to qualify. She failed to check out their rules of lineage, which require *direct* descendancy. Or consider the woman who found an ancestor in a 1760 document with the letters *MD* following his name. She was ecstatic to have found a doctor. However, at that time, *MD* stood for mule driver. She had to be convinced that mule drivers were mighty important persons in those times.

Nobility didn't usually migrate, so there's little use looking in Old World records. And many of the early American settlers fled to escape political or religious persecution, burning evidence as well as their bridges behind them. Anonymity was often a matter of life or death.

In your search, you may need to put aside moral compunctions. One genealogy teacher says every family tree has at least one bastard in the crop, biologically speaking. Other varieties of ancestors may rear their heads—a few of which were chopped off, or may have been. Some people delight in the rogues, pirates, and marauders found among some of the most illustrious family dynasties. Others find bugle boys or indentured servants unacceptable, but there may be one at the end of a direct bloodline, so be prepared.

Another problem is families whose ties were severed on the Western trails to California and Oregon. Special societies have made special studies of these groups.

The most time-consuming problem is locating records or hard data. But the good news is that there is an abundance. Consider, first, which are important to your story, or you may find yourself in a paralyzing network. A few resources are: census records, birth, death, marriage, judicial and civic, court depositories, jury duty, pension and job applications, family bibles, school, military, church, local history, vintage newspapers, records of immigrant ships.

This brings us to the intricate problem of ethnic and recent immigrant records. Thirty million immigrants flooded America's shores after the 1880s. Tracing them is quite different from tracing Anglo-Saxon heritage.

We've become aware of the lineage problems of black slaves, listed among property records, not as people. There were also whites sold and traded into indentured service. Eastern Europeans were allowed to enter, then exploited in sweatshops, while families often scattered to find work. A special problem is the bigotry of the officials of the time in regard to their names and customs. Names were distorted, and many family names were erased by a sweep of the pen. American or Americanized names were substituted. Somehow, my own family name, Konikow, got through intact—but my father changed it later because my brothers complained that the kids in school made fun of it with jibes like "What kind of a cow is a Konikow?"

Birth dates and ages were often changed. One reason, for Jewish immigrants, was the custom of wives being older than their husbands. In some cases he was a scholar and the woman worked. Such an age difference was considered improper in this country.

The descendants of all these people have become interested in their histories only recently, and material on these backgrounds are piling up rapidly.

Collect your data according to the pattern of your story. It's a matter of the mass of material, its amount and type, fitting with a dominant idea.

Decide how much time and effort you want to invest in the search for your roots. Lay out a master plan and a deadline. You can easily get sidetracked or addicted and your book postponed indefinitely. Whatever experience you have, it will confirm the fact that everyone's story, especially yours—to you—has depth, excitement, and much to say and share.

EXERCISE 1. DISTANT RELATIVES

PURPOSE OF THIS EXERCISE

To gather source material when you have out-of-town relatives with whom there has been little or no contact. This exercise is to break the ice.

INSTRUCTIONS

Compose a form letter. Keep it simple. It's a query, just to test the climate: how they feel about you; if they thought about you at all.

EXAMPLE (A HOMEMAKER, AGE FORTY-SEVEN, TO A PATERNAL COUSIN):

Dear Frank,

I know this will be a surprise to you. Our contact through the years has been scant, to say the least.

I'll get right to the point. Through a project I've been working on—specifically, autobiographical writing—I've come to realize that one of the voids in my life has been lack of contact with family. This is an attempt to rectify the situation. I've had a growing need to know more about my father and his family, where they are and what they are doing.

If you are willing to help me put the pieces together, I'd be so happy to hear from you. There is a simple questionnaire I've prepared. Please let me know if I can send it to you.

I may be driving across the country this summer, and if you and Anna will be around, perhaps we can meet.

Here's an instant history of me: Married in 1952, widowed in 1965. I have two children: Robert, eighteen, studying music at the University of California at Irvine; Cindy, married, works for a real estate firm and has one daughter aged four (Tina). I teach school, junior high, and am a Sunday painter, but a serious one.

When I know what interests you, I'll fill in more information. Maybe you could send me a questionnaire for specific information. I'm writing to you first, and would appreciate other names and addresses you can share with me.

Fondly,
Jane

EXERCISE 2. QUESTIONNAIRE ——————————

PURPOSE OF THIS EXERCISE

This is the follow-up to Exercise 1. There could be a series of questionnaires, seeking new information each time.

INSTRUCTIONS

Make this first one simple. Most people hate filling out long forms. After the person replies, you will know better how to structure the following ones.

EXAMPLE (JANE'S FOLLOW-UP LETTER TO FRANK):

> *Dear Frank,*
>
> *Here is the questionnaire I promised:*
>
> 1. *Your birth date, place, and something about the event of your birth—any anecdotes?*
>
> 2. *Who are the other members of your family? What are they doing now?*
>
> 3. *Any early memories of our families getting together?*
>
> 4. *Early memories of our personal contact. Can you remember your first impression of me? What was I like? What did I look like? How did you feel about me?*
>
> *(Note: Please don't hold back any impressions just because they were negative. If you thought I was spoiled or stupid, tell about it or whatever your honest feelings about me were at that time. Don't be afraid of hurting my feelings because any information is important to me so that I may understand myself and my life.)*
>
> 5. *What do you remember about my parents, brothers and sisters?*
>
> 6. *Any special anecdotes come to mind?*

READINGS AND RESOURCES

BOOKS

CASE, PATRICIA ANN. *How to Write Your Autobiography, or Preserving Your Family Heritage.* Santa Barbara, Calif.: Woodbridge Press Publishing Co., 1977. A small book, with simple-to-follow lists as guides to organizing questionnaires for gathering family history data.

DIXON, J. T., and FLACK, D. D. *Preserving Your Past.* Garden City, N.Y.: Doubleday & Co., 1977. A thorough and detailed guide, especially for family history, with many examples.

DOANE, GILBERT H. *Searching for Your Ancestors.* Minneapolis: University of Minnesota Press, 1977. A great little book, full of examples, tips, and anecdotes.

DRAZNIN, YAFFA. *The Family Historian's Handbook.* New York: Harcourt Brace Jovanovich, 1978. A comprehensive book on the problems of tracing your roots, whatever your ethnic background. Especially helpful to those who stem from the later immigration.

HALEY, ALEX. *Roots.* See Readings, Chapter 2, for notes.

SKALKA, L. M. *Tracing, Charting, and Writing Your Family History.* New York: Pilot Books, 1978. An easy guide for beginners.

FAMILY HISTORY OR GENEALOGY SEARCH

U.S. Government Printing Office, Washington, DC 20402. Has pamphlets on where to write for various records.

U.S. Department of Health, Education, and Welfare, National Center for Health Statistics, 5600 Fishers Lane, Room 8-20, Rockville, MD 20852. You may write for books such as *Where to Look for Birth and Death Records* and others, listed state by state. For the serious searcher.

Public libraries. If your local library is not large enough to house a substantial collection or support a genealogy room, they will direct you to the closest one that does. They usually have instruction sheets on how to do your research, and will provide microfilm readers. Interlibrary loan privileges with major city libraries are generally available. Librarians are often genealogy buffs and very helpful.

Genealogy Library of the Church of Jesus Christ of the Latter-Day Saints (the Mormon church), based in Salt Lake City, Utah. The largest library of its kind in the world. Worldwide branches are open to the public and the staff is well trained in the search process. Will also provide names of professionals. For name of nearest branch write: Mormon Church Genealogical Library, 50 East North Temple St., Salt Lake City, UT 84150.

University libraries. Open to the public, although free loan privileges are usually limited to students. Others pay an annual fee. In the reference section, usually on the main floor, will be referral material for the Library of Congress. Check your family surname in all the possible ways it may have been spelled, and all the geographical areas covering your research needs.

National Archives. The Washington base has several branches around the country, and an excellent guidebook. Write for information to National Archives, Washington, DC 20408.

Local churches and clubs. Many of these are for special nationalities, and have regular club meetings or groups concerned with tracing roots and building ethnic pride. Some churches have lunches and dinners after services to preserve ethnic food. There is almost always someone who is well versed in the special sources for racial roots.

LIBRARY SUPPLY MATERIALS FOR ORGANIZING RECORDS

Brodart, Inc., 1609 Memorial Ave., Williamsport, PA 17701. Will send a catalog with colored photographs of most of their supplies, the type of equipment used by libraries, from bookshelf systems to repairing kits for books and pamphlets. Well worth looking into for storing, organizing, and preserving your documents.

Demco Inc., Box 7488, Madison, WI 53701. Same type of material as Brodart, slightly different designs.

6

The Subliminal Self

*One sometimes feels that the unconscious
is leading the way in accordance with
a secret design.*

—M. L. VON FRANZ

There are four major reasons for this chapter:

1. To persuade you that your life is an unfolding of a pattern and a purpose, and to survey your material in this light. When you recognize it, you will see your story in its unity and uniqueness.

2. To help you see your life in its totality, by showing you how to extract material underlying your immediate consciousness and to integrate it.

3. To supply you with techniques to help you reach this subliminal self and to tap latent resources of your mind for the deeper truths. These may be the most important.

4. To aid you further in your search for self-understanding by a tour of psychological knowledge of the human mind and human behavior.

Most of us live with fragments of memories, missing pages in our own histories, and some hazy, half-forgotten events that lurk around the corners of recollections, afraid to come out of hiding. Half-memories are often half-truths.

You may not like the idea of having a subconscious mind.* If so, simply think of this concept as another region of the mind, a storage chamber or mental closet similar to the household variety in which we tuck away things we don't need right now, unsightly possessions, junk we don't know what to do with but can't bring ourselves to throw away, and a skeleton or two.

Somewhere in your psyche is a storehouse of information about everything that ever happened to you, and it's yours for the pickings.

Through this expedition into your subconscious, you may find that portions of your life not previously mentioned in your story, are now essential to your life's design. Submerged parts, once emerged, change this design and give it new meaning. Willingness to accept all of yourself is important to mental health, as well as to an interesting story.

New schools of psychology are cropping up as fast as we can read books about them. To avoid getting stuck in a quagmire of theories, rely on your sense of intuition and choose theories you like. Following are thumbnail sketches of a few.

DEFENSE MECHANISMS

We all know what it is to be "on the defensive," but this usually refers to something we do deliberately, knowingly. But as postulated by Sigmund Freud, defense mechanisms are devices used subconsciously to ward off anxiety, the psychological counterpart of physical pain. Both are necessary to warn us of danger—that something needs attention and care. Understanding this process helps the autobiographer to confront material that he has been avoiding. But these devices appear in life as blocks to growth. If you suspect you have had these, check out the possibility of one or more of them in operation. We tend to adopt favorites. Here are a few basic ones which you may recognize:

*I'll use the term *subconscious* though some prefer *unconscious,* used by Jung. He felt that the Freudian prefix *sub* suggested "inferior." *Subconscious* is better known.

Repression—the basic defense out of which all others are derived. Feelings, memories, desires, and ideas that are too painful to handle are stuffed down into the subconscious. We are not conscious of this process, or of the moment we made the decision to turn away from a reality. But it remains latent, like a time bomb.

Denial—denying an act or state of being, a form of lying to ourselves and others. The lie is what we prefer to believe. For example, a person to whom illness is unacceptable will deny there is anything wrong, even if he is sneezing, coughing, and running a high fever. He will say, "No, no, I'm all right, just a little dust in the air."

Reaction formation—subconsciously eliminating something painful by adopting *opposite* behavior. A classic example is the overprotective mother who goes to extremes in caring for her children, when she really hates the job. It is unacceptable to her moral conditioning to be less than enthusiastic about motherhood.

Projection—Things we can't cope with are projected, or thrown at someone else like a hot potato. As example, a minister with strong sex urges that are against his principles accuses others of chronic lust.

Rationalization, withdrawal, fixation, and martyrdom—are a few generally familiar defenses worth checking out in your own history, and other characters in your life story.

JUNG'S FOUR FUNCTIONS

C. G. Jung's theory of personality is based on polarity, or opposites, in our nature. He refers to four basic functions, represented in this diagram:

Thinking—the intellectual capacity.

Feeling—experiencing emotions, evaluating people and things in relation to ourselves and how we feel about them.

Sensation—reality experience through the five senses.

Intuition—experiences of the "sixth" sense.

The purpose is to achieve a balance of all four. All are inherent and necessary, but one usually dominates and can throw the rest off balance, causing the others to be "inferior." A classic example is the "egghead" or scientist who develops his intellect to a high degree but neglects his feeling function at the expense of warm human relationships.

How does your personality fit this diagram? Were you imbalanced at some point? Did you become more balanced? How?

BERNE'S TRANSACTIONAL ANALYSIS

Eric Berne, author of *Games People Play*, developed a perspective on personality called Transactional Analysis, popularly known as TA. As we transact with others, we use three basic "ego states," observable visibly and audibly by gestures, tone of voice, body language, and so on.

Parent ego state—the voice of authority. What we learn by rote from society, parents, teachers. Words like *should, ought, bad, silly, proper*, etc., are Parent words. The pointed finger is a typical gesture. Judgmental and punitive behavior. The good Parent is the nurturing one whose motives are not toward gaining control.

Adult ego state—our practical, unemotional, thinking part that deals with up-to-date facts, acquired skills. The computer or machine part that we need to do our work and transact with others realistically.

Child ego state—our mad/glad/sad emotional side. The natural curious inner child filled with the wonder of the world, able to have fun and excitement.

We need all three of these ego states, but to function at effective times and places. One state usually dominates the personality. One can be contaminated by another. An example is a person who is conditioned to take care of others and will often relate to a spouse this way at all times, neglecting the "fun kid" when it's time for sex or mutually enjoyed relaxation activities.

Which state dominates your personality? How has it manifested itself in your life?

MASLOW'S SELF-ACTUALIZATION

Abraham Maslow was the first psychologist to study personality through mentally healthy people instead of the mentally ill. He researched the lives of great achievers to discover what made them so and found a hierarchy of human needs that were being fulfilled.

First are *basic survival needs* such as hunger, security, affection, and self-esteem.

Beyond these are *metaneeds,* such as justice, goodness, beauty, and order. If they are unfulfilled, the consequences are dangerous to mental health and happiness—alienation, anguish, apathy, cynicism.

At the summit are *peak experiences,* described in different ways by those who have had them: feeling of exaltation, bliss, oneness with the universe, presence of God, complete happiness.

Which of these needs have been fulfilled or thwarted in your life? Which do you relate to now, positively or negatively?

BEHAVIOR MODIFICATION

The general public knows of behavior modification or behaviorism through the work of B. F. Skinner, the author of *Walden Two.* Critics are primarily opposed to its *reductionist* approach that reduces people to "nothing but a machine."

The fact is that a part of us does function like a machine and can be trained or "conditioned" like a robot to do almost anything. This training can bypass our conscious minds, free will, moral sense, and spiritual qualities.

We are conditioned already whether we like it or not, believe it or not. If you think you understand yourself fully, check out some of your preferences in the light of their origin. For example, one student who "ate to live" and disliked dealing with food, discovered it was because mealtime was the arena of all family disputes when she was growing up. She had never connected the two. This valuable information evolved from writing her autobiography, and helped her understand the battles with a husband who badgered her because of her unwillingness to learn to cook. You may love popcorn without knowing why. You may have been programmed by a machine. As far back as 1956, the Subliminal Projection Company proved that directive messages can be given without the subject's knowledge. For six weeks in a theater in New Jersey, a message was flashed on the screen at given intervals: "Eat Popcorn." The experimenters and happy popcorn vendors watched the sale of popcorn increase 57 percent!

Needless to say, behavior modification is a powerful tool in the wrong hands. But the good news is that conditioned behavior can be reversed by use of the same tools.

ASSERTIVENESS TRAINING

Behavior can become lopsided and swing from assertive to passive or aggressive. Assertiveness training is an outgrowth of behavior modification. It was found that anxiety was related to passivity. Techniques were developed to reverse the process, to cure anxiety.

Table 6.1 encapsulates the three basic behavior types: passive, assertive, and aggressive.

Don't let this view of behavior scare you. No one is 100 percent passive or aggressive, and we are all assertive to a degree. We mix these up at different times and places. A man may be aggressive at the office, assertive toward his wife, and passive with his mother.

A common mistake is to confuse assertiveness with aggressiveness. You can't be too assertive. If it seems that way, you've slipped into aggressiveness.

Check yourself out through your life's story in terms of some major relationships. Many people are stunned by the realization that they have allowed themselves to be manipulated by aggressive people (or by one in particular), or that they have acted aggressively at some time.

Were there long-lasting habit patterns or attitudes you changed along the way? Did you fail to stick up for your rights or get your needs answered? Did you learn how to get help when you needed it, and to receive help comfortably?

Assertiveness is important here because it is based on self-

TABLE 6.1. THE THREE BASIC BEHAVIOR TYPES

PASSIVE	ASSERTIVE	AGGRESSIVE
Receives or endures without resistance. Self-denying. Inhibited. Fixed ideas. Acts by rote, myths, assumptions. Easily swayed. Puts self down.	Acts in own interests and gets needs met without hurting others or denying their rights. Expresses needs, feelings, opinions without anxiety. Spontaneous. Puts self and others up. Nonjudgmental, accepting.	Masquerades as assertive. Indifferent to needs, rights, and feelings of others. Manipulates, dominates. Rigid ideas. Prejudiced.
Acts like a loser. Goals not defined or achieved. Waits for others to give or do for them.	Achiever. Self-productive. Noncompetitive. Cooperative.	Achieves by exploiting others. Intensely competitive. Uses. Takes credit for work done by others.
Lets others choose. Looks to authorities to make decisions. Tentative. Procrastinates. Spins wheels. Pessimistic. Negative.	Assertiveness leads to brevity. Doesn't play games. Comes on straight but with kindness, discretion, and effective timing.	Hard game player. Interrupts and finishes sentences for others. Controls conversation. Inhibits others' expression.
Consequences: Feels guilty, anxious, or stupid. Becomes repressed. Periodically explodes into anger, violence: ineffective aggression. *Response from others:* Pity, contempt, indifference, boredom. *Response to others:* Envy, inferior by comparison, resentment.	*Results:* Makes friends easily. Not afraid of intimacy. Generates admiration, trust. Inspires good relationships. Benefits by understanding of others and enjoys their differences.	*Consequences:* Few or no intimate relationships. Superficial friendships, based on gain. Generates resentment, hatred, revenge from victims. Underlying guilt. Contempt for others. Blocks love. Short-sighted. Wants what you and everyone else has. Is never satisfied.

esteem. You are writing a book about yourself. You are the heroine or hero. You are in the spotlight. Give yourself permission to care enough about yourself to study and describe yourself. Feel worthy enough to share this information, this story, with many others. Feel worthy of recognition and admiration.

RELAXATION, CONCENTRATION, SELF-HYPNOSIS, MEDITATION

These techniques are separate and different, but related. They will help you gather material that doesn't come easily off the top of your head or desk. Many people have neglected to document events, but none of these events are gone forever. They are recorded in your subconscious and can be recovered.

If you don't need to delve into the deeper regions of your mind or don't like the idea, you can just latch on to relaxation techniques. They will at least be good for your health and expand your memory bank. Relaxation invites undercover thoughts and feelings we hold back by tensing up.

The British poet Edward Muir said: "I think there must be a mind within our mind which cannot rest until it has worked out, even against our conscious will, the unresolved questions of the past."

Relaxation is the use of the conscious mind for the body's ability to release tension. *Concentration* is the use of the conscious mind to focus on one thing at a time. *Self-hypnosis* starts with a state of relaxation to drift into a mental state in which the conscious mind is rendered inactive as the controller of behavior, and the subconscious mind is allowed to direct behavior with the conscious mind in the background as monitor. *Meditation* is a state in which the conscious and subconscious minds are inactivated. The purpose here is to allow the self to be directed from within the superconscious, the deepest self, the core, the center of self or soul, depending on your philosophy.

These skills can be acquired by anyone willing to spend a measure of time and effort.

RELAXATION

This skill needs to be *relearned*. Babies don't have to be taught to relax. As we grow older, tensions appear. The meaning of life is too often overpowered by frenetic survival and pressures of competition. Relaxation is the way back to self and sanity and is a vital tool for the autobiographer who needs to define and build a self-image.

Here is a simple way to begin developing this skill:

Lie down, preferably on an exercise mat on the floor, or any place comfortable to you. Wear loose clothing. The room should be dim. If necessary for warmth, use a light coverlet. You can prop up your knees, elbows, and neck with small pillows or rolled towels.

With eyes closed, draw an imaginary line between your mind and your *left big toe*. Focus on the feeling of tension there. When you have caught even the tiniest tension, become aware of the holding device causing the tension, and *release it*. If you have trouble letting it go, tense the tight spot as hard as you can, then let go—all the way.

This back-and-forth movement is exactly like training a muscle to strengthen it and gain control over it.

Do the same with the *right big toe*, left little toe, right, then left, calf muscles, under knee, upper calf, buttocks, fingers, lower arm, upper arm, chest, neck, right and left shoulder. Linger on your facial muscles—jaw, eyes, forehead, ears, nose.

When you look into a mirror, notice your habits of facial tensions that distort your features. This will help enormously when you study old photographs. Become aware of your body movements in relation to tension and study your old pictures to see when and how these developed.

CONCENTRATION

This ability, perhaps more than any other, is mentioned as a key factor in the success stories of achievers. People who were single-minded toward a goal were able to visualize that goal, making distractions evaporate, and the clear goal materialize. Einstein was a master of this skill. His door was always open to students who drifted in and out, allowed to interrupt his work. He felt that he could return at any time to a point of concentration.

Try a simple exercise. Try doing it at the same time every day. Start with as little as five minutes, and work it up to fifteen. The object will be to focus your mind on a single thought or image for progressively longer periods.

Sit comfortably. Choose an image or idea. Focus on it. When diverted by inner or outer distractions, *go with* them for a few moments, then bring your thoughts back gently to the image.

When your session is finished, make a list of distractions with comments on them. They supply interesting material for future use in your book. You can choose any image of the past, something you need to clarify or complete. The inner distractions will give you information about it or insight into what may be blocking your memory.

SELF-HYPNOSIS

As noted before, the subconscious mind is activated and the conscious mind stays in the background as monitor. This is important to know because a common myth is the fear that a hypnotist can control someone's mind. All hypnosis is in effect self-hypnosis, and is self-monitored. You will not do things that are against your principles. If you are in danger while in a hypnotic state or a child cries out for you, the conscious mind will call you back to take care of whatever is important and appropriate to you.

If the autobiographer learns self-hypnosis, the subconscious mind can be persuaded to release any of its stored information and secrets. People under hypnosis have "become" three years old, exactly as if they were projected back into time, with voice and gestures, and can recall "lost" events.

Confusions about your past, for example, reasons for decisions you made, reactions to others, repressed traumas, and simple information like names, dates, and places, are all within recall under hypnosis.

Hypnosis can also be used to develop discipline in setting up a schedule. It can help you develop the courage to write and keep going. If it is developed to a high level, you can recall letters received or sent—verbatim—past conversations, anything. Jacques Cousteau tells of his aged father who sat up in his deathbed and recited his entire doctoral dissertation! There are a few simple rules for effective self-hypnosis:

1. *Use the present tense.* Instead of saying "I must relax," say "I am relaxed and calm." If you wish to recall a past event, discuss it as if it were happening *now*.

2. *Be positive.* Don't use negative terms such as "I won't be afraid." Instead say, "I am courageous."

3. *Use specifics.* Work on one thing at a time.

4. Visualize goals in every possible detail as you describe your wishes. If you are trying to understand a past relationship, go over it and ask for information in every detailed way.

5. Put a charge into your words and images. Express your desires with emotion and excitement.

6. Square off with reality. Be honest. Use valid data. Don't cheat. You can't fool your subconscious.

7. Work on yourself, not on others.

MEDITATION

Other techniques deal primarily with information and mechanics. Meditation is practiced for understanding and for the development of intuitive and creative powers. It holds the master key to self-understanding, the foundation of successful autobiography. Its main purpose is to help you tap the wellspring of your story's theme and your uniqueness by tapping your inner self.

Varieties of techniques are ubiquitous. I only hope to whet your appetite with a simple introductory exercise. First, there is no single correct way to meditate. Even postures vary. You can be lying down, sitting, standing, twirling, or chanting.

A surprising number of high achievers say they could not make it through the day or accomplish what they do without a half hour of quiet time to themselves every day. So let's take a half hour as a good average time.

Be aware of the usual activity of your mind. The Hindus describe it as a "skittering monkey," and Saint Teresa of Avila pictured it as an "unbroken horse that would go anywhere except where you want it to." It is this tendency you will be working on. There are two basic steps. The first is to quiet the mind. The second is to get the mind out of the way.

To quiet the mind, a simple beginning is to sit in a comfortable position at a time and a place where you are not likely to be interrupted. Select an image. For your project you can even select an image of your book as you would like to see it finished. If you are spiritually inclined, you can envision it surrounded by white light or held by a spiritual figure. Or you can visualize yourself in an ideal state. Use any symbol that feels right. Flowers, trees, and lakes are favorites to inspire beauty and peace. With eyes closed or half-closed, use the concentration exercise, bringing the mind back gently each time it wanders. This time let the distractions go without thinking about them. When you can hold the image for a manageable length of time (even a few seconds), go to the second step.

Now set the image in the background as you relax into the *feeling* of it. Focus gently on awareness of the experience of being this image and feel it. After a while, you will *just be.* This is the ultimate state in which you will be receptive to whatever your inner self will reveal. Don't wait for words. Meanings and ideas will come which you will translate later into words.

Meditation is totally personal. But there is a common component, difficult to describe. At a conference of psychologists who meditated, one gave an answer as to why they did it—an answer that satisfied them all. He said: "It's like coming home."

What better goal for the autobiographer?

DREAMS

The mystery of this mental phenomenon has been pondered down through history. It's been called everything from God's forgotten language to a garbage pail of repressed wishes. Ancient and biblical peoples relied on dreams for guidance, and scientists today are penetrating more of their secrets. Theories of interpretation vary, but most agree that the final interpretation rests with the dreamer.

While working on your book, you will probably be dreaming of things related to it as you dredge up memories. We all dream, but not all of us remember our dreams. Why not use this deep area of the mind to help with information and understanding? Dreams are sources of wisdom, inspiration, and solutions.

Using your new skills of relaxation, before you go to sleep at night, focus on a problem of your past and ask your dream self to send you an answer. Try this even if it feels silly. Persistence will bring results. Recollecting and gathering dreams is a skill you can develop. Here are a few fundamental points:

1. Before going to sleep, direct yourself to remember your dreams when you awake. Be confident this will happen.

2. Dreams fade quickly, so record them quickly on awakening. Write down or tape-record them.

3. Write the dream using the present tense. It's more vivid that way.

4. Include every possible detail, even if it doesn't seem to be important. Everything in a dream is.

5. Train yourself to recall unpleasant dreams you might otherwise block out. You will realize that they are not to be feared, but are ways of transferring strong information or getting your attention.

Interpreting dreams is another skill you can learn. As you collect them, you may notice repetitive images. These are powerful messages directing you to important areas to work on. Dreams contain a balancing factor. Areas we have neglected will appear and bug us until we do something about them. Remember, all parts of a dream represent a quality of the self. Here are some guidelines:

1. Take a dream, or a fragment. What comes to mind about its meaning? If you get a speeding ticket in one dream, it may have a simple meaning of the need to slow down some activity.

2. Become any symbol, person, or object you don't understand. If you are puzzled about why your long-dead father appears, does it suggest that you want to be taken care of or protected? Or that he doesn't approve of something you are doing? Your father as a symbol of self may be saying, "I'm facing a scary situation," or "My conscience is bothering me."

3. Be totally aware of the *feeling* of the image. Explore all shades of those feelings and how they relate to something in your waking life.

4. Make note of colors and what they mean to you. Do the same with numbers.

5. Describe backgrounds and scenery. They tell us how we experience our environment and the world.

6. Think in symbolic terms. Animals many represent qualities of your development or an aspect of personality. Death may signal something you are letting go of, or the end of a phase of your life.

7. Take the dream to a conclusion in terms of what you need to finish or understand more fully.

Don't let this whirlwind tour of psychology intimidate you. Use what you can, leave the rest, and pursue further through reading and classes what is most useful. As an autobiographer, you will find the pursuit of self to be your most exciting activity.

EXERCISE: SAMPLE TAPE FOR SELF-HYPNOSIS

This exercise is for those who wish to make a self-hypnosis tape to practice induction. If read slowly, each page will take about three minutes, making the following a ten-minute tape. You may want to extend it to a half-hour tape, adding material of your own. Beginners usually need a half hour; after that, they can shorten it to ten minutes, and later just a cue word will do it.

Use your own voice when you are in a positive and relaxed mood. You can also use a commercial tape, or if you have a friend whose voice is persuasive or pleasant to you, ask her or him to read your copy. Use the sample below or compose your own "lullaby" to suit your specific needs. Allow generous pauses.

Refresh yourself on the key points in making the most effective tape:

1. Use the present tense.

2. Be positive.

3. Use specifics.

4. Visualize goals in detail.

5. Work only on yourself, not others.

There are three parts to a tape: (1) a relaxation exercise to induce the hypnotic state; (2) a message to your subconscious to work on a specific task; (3) You may want to include a posthypnotic suggestion at the very end.

SAMPLE TAPE

Get comfortable . . . be sure your clothing is loose . . . stretch . . . strrreetch all over . . . yawn . . . relax . . . reeelaaaxx . . . your eyes are heavy . . . eyelids are heevvyy . . . let them drop . . . close your eyes . . . breathe deeply . . . be aware of your breathing . . . how it goes in . . . how it goes out . . . feel more relaxed with each breath . . . with each exhalation a little more tension melts away . . . feeling warm and wonderful . . . you are lying on the warm sand of a beautiful beach . . . warm breezes embrace you . . .

(long pause)

be aware of your left little toe, then the right one . . . feel the slightest tension in them . . . move them slightly to know that you can control them, one at a time, then let them go . . . mo-o-or-r-re-e . . . be aware of your ankles . . . let them go-o-o-o . . . the calf of you left leg . . . tense it a little and let it go . . . more . . . more . . . your knees . . . let go . . . more . . . breathe deeply, letting out all the tensions from your knees down . . . feel the tension in the front of your lower leg, first the left, then the right one . . . tense them one at a time by raising the leg slightly to get in touch with its specific muscle . . . now let it go . . . let it go more . . . your legs are beginning to tingle . . . they are twitching . . . it's warm and wonderful . . . concentrate on relaxing your abdomen . . . your solar plexis is at the upper part of your abdomen . . . feel it soften and let it go, releasing any soreness or tightness . . . soothing . . . soothing . . . breathe deeply into your solar plexis . . . relax with every exhalation . . . do this several times . . . slowly . . . slowly . . .

(long pause)

feel your lower back respond to the gentle waves of relaxation that are now floating through your body . . . become aware of your buttocks, your genitals . . . there are little tensions . . . hold them a moment and let them go . . . more . . . more . . . once more . . . you are totally relaxed from the waist down . . . your eyes are growing heavier and heavier . . . your shoulders and neck are a little tense . . . release them . . . again . . . deeper . . . deeper . . . your face feels tense . . . release it . . . release subtle tensions behind your eyes . . . lips . . . tongue . . . chin . . . cheeks . . . ears . . . scalp . . . all at once let al-l-l-l those go-o-o-o . . . deeper . . . deeper . . . concentrate on your upper arms . . . tensing the muscle and letting it go . . . there's a tiny bit more tension there . . . let it go . . . gooooo . . . do the same for your lower arms . . . release it . . . notice the little tension points in your fingers . . . relax your left pinky . . . a little more . . . from left to right, take each finger at a time and let the tensions go . . . one . . . two . . . three . . . four . . . five . . . six . . . seven . . . eight . . . nine . . . ten . . . your body is limp and loose . . . limp and loose . . . you are floating . . . floating . . . you are completely calm . . . soooo goooood . . . so relaxed . . . all muscles are sinking . . . sagging . . . drooping . . . fading . . . there is only a beautiful feeling of calm . . . serenity . . . peace . . . peace . . . peace . . .

(pause)

in this lovely state you are more aware of your selfness than ever before . . . you are *you* . . . you are special and unique . . . you are happy to be you . . . accepting all of you . . . accepting everything that ever happened to you as part of a plan . . . as necessary to your growth . . . you will explore the hidden messages in all the events of your life . . . you will recall the joys . . . you will remember everything you need to know . . . you will go back as far as you wish . . . taking all of life's experience, joys, and sorrows as part of what made you as you are . . . all necessary to bring you to this point of understanding . . . taking all the events of your life with the wisdom and the kindness of the adult that you are today . . . forgive yourself for all the things you don't like about your behavior . . . forgive others who have hurt you . . . forgive them all . . . this is necessary for your growth . . . all resentments fade away with your tensions . . . you can no longer feel hatred toward anyone . . . bad feelings are poisons to you . . . let them go . . .

(pause)

when you get up tomorrow morning, you will go to your desk . . . feeling enthusiastic about your project . . . you will outline the day's work . . . you will make a schedule . . . then you will start your day . . . feeling wonderful . . . feeling content with your past . . . feeling hopeful for the future . . .

(pause)

at the count of ten you will stretch slowly . . . open your eyes . . . return to the now . . . one . . . two . . . three . . . four . . . five . . . six . . . seven . . . eight . . . nine . . . ten.

READINGS

PSYCHOLOGICAL TECHNIQUES

ALBERTI, ROBERT E., Ph. D., and EMMONS, MICHAEL L., Ph.D. *Your Perfect Right.* San Luis Obispo, Calif.: Impact, Box 1094, 93406, 1974. My own favorite among the vast numbers of books on assertiveness training. This was the original.

BERNE, ERIC, M.D. *Games People Play.* New York: Grove Press, 1967. Also *Transactional Analysis in Psychotherapy.* New York: Grove Press, 1961. Eric Berne's psychological system of self-understanding using plain language and shortcuts to getting at solutions.

EVANS, RICHARD I. *B. F. Skinner: The Man and His Ideas.* New York: E. P. Dutton, 1968. A simple-to-understand book explaining Skinner's contributions to behavior modification and how it works.

FREUD, SIGMUND. *The Basic Writings of Sigmund Freud.* Translated and edited with an Introduction by A. A. Brill. New York: Random House, 1938. For those interested in pursuing the study of psychoanalysis.

JUNG, CARL GUSTAV. *Man and His Symbols.* Garden City, N. Y.: Doubleday & Co., 1964. A beautiful book, profusely illustrated with color photographs and paintings. The best way I know of being introduced to the deep concepts of Jung in a well-written series of articles by some of his followers and colleagues.

MASLOW, ABRAHAM H. *Toward a Psychology of Being.* Princeton, N.J.: D. Van Nostrand Co., 1968. Maslow's humanistic approach is extremely interesting and optimistic, and well written. Self-actualization is the goal here.

TRAINING THE MIND

BAKER, M. E. PENNY. *Meditation: A Step Beyond with Edgar Cayce.* New York: Pinnacle Books, 1973. A fascinating book with excerpts from the readings of the famous mystic.

BENSON, HERBERT, M.D. *The Relaxation Response.* New York; Avon Books, 1975. For those who prefer a more scientific approach to the subject of reaching the deeper recesses of the mind.

FARADAY, ANN. *The Dream Game.* New York: Harper & Row, 1976. Also *Dream Power.* New York: Coward, McCann & Geoghegan, 1972. A popular and thorough coverage of the subject, with techniques and helpful basics for those who wish to learn how to interpret their own dreams.

FINK, DAVID HAROLD, M.D. *Release from Nervous Tension.* New York: Simon & Schuster, 1962. One of the early books on the subject, and still one of the best.

PARAMPANTHI, SWAMI. *Creative Self-Transformation Through Meditation.* Astara's Library of Mystical Classics, Los Angeles, CA, 90004. A very practical system of learning to meditate, step by step, outlined in a course. Geared to the Western mind. An excellent and clearly written book.

SECHRIST, ELSIE. *Dreams, Your Magic Mirror.* New York: Warner Books, 1974. Interpretations by Edgar Cayce of dreams in his collection of readings. Self-understanding on a spiritual level.

SHATTOCK, E. H. *An Experiment in Mindfulness.* New York: E. P. Dutton, 1960. An Englishman's search for more meaning in life through a stay in a Buddhist monastery in Rangoon, Burma, where he learned the Satipatthana training in mind control.

7

Diaries, Journals, and Other Raw Material

*We want inner peace but we
will not look within.*

—MATTHEW ARNOLD

Diary or journal writing has entered the writing scene with the impact of a cult. Classes and books multiply like rabbits. You may have a basement full of trunks overflowing with diaries, as many do, or you may not yet have succumbed to this form of self-expression.

The diary is a form in itself, not to be confused with autobiography. I don't mean to belittle it by calling it raw material, but it is just that for writing an autobiographical story.

Raw material is not limited to the written word. Photographs, artwork, letters, or anything can be integrated into the story. You select the material you need for your story, and avoid getting bogged down with all the details of your life.

The diary provides references and helps keep a chronological record of your inner and outer life. Its deepest function is to penetrate the surface you to the whole and real and clarified you. Rereading past diaries is a special experience, and even more specialized when done for the focus of your book. You can direct your ongoing, present diary toward probing fuzzy areas of the past.

But I warn you, a diary can become an addiction. It can be a positive addiction if your writer's x-ray vision is used to detect more and more previously unsuspected life material. And if your primary purpose is self-understanding, the diary is the authentic way to achieve it in the long run. The future of therapeutic technique is in developing methods of *autotherapy*. The diary is fundamental to this concept. And the price is right.

There is some confusion about the difference between a diary and a journal. Both stem from a Latin root meaning "day." Occasionally you will see it called a log or memoir. Call it whatever feels best to you. To me, *diary* feels more personal. *Log* is associated in my mind with ships, and *journal* with newspapers and the specialized Progoff Intensive Journal (see page 102). For simplicity's sake, I'll use *diary* in this book. You can even give it a name. Anne Frank called hers Kitty as an imaginary friend and confidante.

More important is your reason for keeping it. Here are a few well-known diarists telling theirs:

> The false person I had created for the enjoyment of my friends, the gaiety, the buoyant, the receptive, the healing person, always on call, always ready with sympathy, had to have its existence somewhere. In the diary I could reestablish the balance. Here I could be depressed, angry, disparaging, discouraged. I could let out my demons. (ANAÏS NIN)

> I wanted to write, but more than that, I wanted to bring out all kinds of things that lie buried deep in my heart. (ANNE FRANK)

> I meant my notebooks to be a storehouse of materials for future use and nothing else. (SOMERSET MAUGHAM. He reduced fifteen notebooks to one, published as *A Writer's Notebook*, a courageous cutting job, to say the least.)

> A diary should simply be. (GERTRUDE STEIN)

Diaries have always been. Teenagers go to them when communication with adults breaks down, and to cope with the wonders and scarinesses of puberty. Men in service have turned to a diary to preserve their emotional balance. Women have written unceasingly throughout history when their channels for expression were blocked, much of this expression dealing with frustrations in love and work.

The diary is a place—physically, psychologically, emotionally, intellectually, and spiritually.

It is a place of respite after an overload.

It is a place of reality for the self, where we can restore our authenticity. No need to perform for others, bend to another's will or need, use devices or guile, adhere to rules. Amenities and defenses can be discarded. At times these may be so built up on our psyches, they need to be scraped off like barnacles.

It is a place where we can release our full range of emotion. We can express our undisguised feelings, holding back nothing for fear of reprisal or hurt.

It is a place to meditate, to clarify our prayers, to commune with our hearts, and invite our souls. We can tend our best selves in their striving toward perfection.

It is a place to allow our fantasies and imagination full power, and to tap the well of creativity.

It is a place of safety and total acceptance where we can practice writing, try out ideas, work out problems, spark our intellect, and expand our mental potential.

It is a place to preserve and conjure up memories that otherwise evaporate.

Let it carry you away, but don't forget to come back. It is only a tool. Take charge of it, and it will make your book richer and fuller. It will help you sort yourself out from others, to see your life as special and important.

Nikos Kazantzakis created Zorba the Greek to display the importance of each person's unique life. One's story is one's life. Zorba says, "When I die, the whole zorbatic world dies with me."

A treasury of material is often shoved away in storage boxes. Among old snapshots, letters, and diaries are other records that don't ordinarily ring bells as research for autobiography, but can supply information to fill in cracks in one's past history.

Old clothes can remind you of changing tastes. Baby clothes fill you in on your mother's taste, or that of whoever bought them for you. You may recall anecdotes about them. Old business records can reveal changing priorities and preoccupations through the years, starting with how we spent our money. How and where we *got* our money tells us much about dependencies and independence, self-image and estimate of our worth, realistic and unrealistic feelings or goals, limitations, and those abilities that brought us monetary recognition.

There are no musts for diary-keeping. Even "authorities" tread softly on the subject of rules. You are on your own. But getting started is often difficult.

The most important factor reported by students is the fear that the God of Literary Excellence is peering over their shoulders. This will keep you from developing your writing potential and moving your life forward. Try out as many systems of diary writing as you can find and devise a simple technique that works for you. When it stops working, examine it and adjust it.

There is no way your entries can be judged right or wrong, good or bad.

For those who want specific guidelines to get started, there are several ways. The Intensive Journal workshops developed by Ira Progoff are considered by some the McDonald's of journal writing, but others swear that the experience transformed their lives. You can work with the text. You keep a notebook with sixteen prearranged headings and write in it when you feel the urge, but it works best when kept on a regular basis. There are "log" sections (factual, outer experiences), and "feedback" sections in which "transformations of awareness" are carried out through inner journeys. Keeping accounts of various portions and aspects of your life, the process is designed to integrate and develop the parts of it into a patterned design—a unique story.

Some of you may wish to design your own headings and invent a system. Tolstoy used a simple method. He kept two diaries, one to record external happenings, the other to interpret the significance of these happenings. From these he fashioned his fictional stories, also his autobiography. Thoreau kept a rough journal as raw material. He polished the first draft, then copied the revision into another notebook. This version was further edited by him. Then he selected passages from the final draft for the book he was writing: the classic *Walden*.

For a positive autobiography, the key is obviously to recall positive things, especially moments of joy. Collect these, and build up your power of positive feelings. Some people, especially older people, when reviewing their past, tend to dwell on mistakes, sorrows, and remorse, thereby distorting memories of a great store of joy available in reexperiencing the past. If it is not nurtured, joy can fade—even fade out. Current events are viewed through a gray screen.

The greatest reward in writing autobiography is feeling O.K. about your whole life. Unless you work at this, you cannot be receptive to the happiness available to you right now. A positive viewpoint will make your book more helpful to yourself and others. Nobody but a disturbed person wants to read a pessimistic book, and it doesn't help to feed into this pessimism. Diaries can turn this around.

If you feel inspired to pursue diary writing, follow up with other books and classes. This is essential if your goal in autobiography is for self-revelation.

A few techniques seem germane here. You want to catch thoughts on the run in addition to sitting down to concentrate. One way is to use a basic $8\frac{1}{2} \times 11$ looseleaf notebook as a catchall. Fleeting feelings and ideas can be captured on restaurant napkins, the backs of matchbooks, or scraps of grocery-bag paper, then pasted or copied in the notebook later.

An alternative is to carry a smaller notebook, about 5×9, in your handbag or attache case, and write everything in it neatly as you go. You can also carry a pocketsize tape recorder. An advantage is that this yields more material. The disadvantage is that transcribing is time-consuming.

Some orthodox diarists insist on a leather- or plastic-bound book with blank pages, so they are not limited as to size of handwriting and can draw pictures or charts and paste or staple in loose items. They say that looseleaf is too tempting for editing, tearing out pages, that it mars the purity of spontaneity.

You can have the best of both diary worlds. Keep a pure diary account, and copy out what you want for your autobiography. I suggest you do this as you go along. If not, you will have the tedious job of combing through the diary in addition to old diaries, letters, and the like.

Orthodox diarists believe in writing longhand, but if you get on a kick about something and ideas are pouring out, you may want to switch to the typewriter. This is one time the looseleaf is more practical.

But you are writing a story and need to organize the parts of your life, so you will need to collect material in an indexed notebook, or file folders, or both. One man wrote his diary in continuity, but used different-colored ink for different areas—blue for dreams, red for emotional problems, and so on. One journal-writing text suggests writing codes in the margins for different subjects, such as *D* for dreams or *Hlt* for health. Play around with materials and mechanics. It's part of the fun.

The diary is like an archeological dig. You never know what the spade or pen will unearth. At times write fast, from your heart and soul, at other times more slowly, from your head. Dump everything into the diary. Later you will go diamond mining to select the material for your book.

The diarist is not bound by scheduled writing, and finds the time when insight is best invoked, or when the spirit moves. But as an autobiographer, remember, you need to function as a writer and write regularly in the book. If you are too busy to record a thought, a memory, or a happening, make a note that will remind you of it, as if you were writing a one-liner or a news headline. Fill it in as soon as you can. Thoughts evaporate rapidly. Unless you have total recall you had better write down everything you may want to use: jokes, emotional impact, first impressions, descriptions. Evenings are a good time to review the day, mornings the times to catch your dreams.

If you have any past diaries, you will be reviewing them. Your Now Self becomes reacquainted with your Then Self—both parts of the real you. Some like to comment within the pages of the old diary with another color of ink—but please try not to criticize your old self or make "corrections." Allow yourself to be imperfect at all times, including the past, and still be O.K. Louisa May Alcott was asked to write a "girl's book" and she refused on the grounds that she did not enjoy this sort of thing, "never liked girls or knew many, except my sisters, but our queer plays and experiences may prove interesting, though I doubt it." Many years later, after *Little Women* was an instant success, she wrote next to that entry, "Good joke." She continued to annotate diary notes as long as forty years later.

It's best to reread old diaries in digestible gulps. While rereading, comments in the old diary or your present one can give a sense of growth and change.

Being aware of your handwriting gives bonus data about how you felt at the time, whether the direction of the writing slanted up or down for emotional swings and whether it was tight and tense, or loose and free.

In some special cases, one could ask another person to make comments. Alcott, on her eleventh birthday, wrote, "I told mother I liked to have her write in my book . . . she wrote this to help me:"

Dear Louy,

Your handwriting improves very fast. Take pains and do not be in a hurry. I like to have you make observations about our conversations and your thoughts. It helps you to express them and to understand your little self. Remember, dear girl, that a diary should be an epitome of your life. May it be a record of pure thought and good actions, then, you will indeed, be the precious child of your loving mother.

Few children these days would be willing, to say the least, to share their diary with their mothers, or ask their help with it, especially at eleven! But whether you agree or not with the surrounding sentiments, the diary can be regarded as the epitome of a life, or its essence.

There is a trend today to share diaries within a group, or with another person. This may require some tempering in cases where entries could be hurtful to others or damaging to a relationship. You may want to keep a separate and secret book, or if you keep one book with everything in it, keep it in a safe place. Even if you live alone, you have the danger of prying visitors. You may even wonder about reactions to the diary in the event of death. Will others be shocked? Hurt? Feel guilty?

Tennessee Williams was asked on a talk show if he had any qualms about "telling all" about his life. Williams, who had referred to himself as a confessional writer, said that telling everything one knows of the truth is the essential responsibility of the writer.

But if you live with someone and don't feel ready to tell all, there are two alternatives: keep the diary itself a secret, or if you must, make an agreement with the others that its privacy is to be honored. In some cases this will require strategy and a great deal of self-control on the part of the others. Someone close to you may be overcome with curiosity or a feeling of being threatened. Consider where they are now in their relationship with you. You may have a "closed" relationship (not open and honest with each other).

But here is a warning, from a therapist's point of view: If you tell others that your diary is somewhere in the house but woe unto those who sneak a peek, take care that your decision doesn't come from defiance. You may find yourself "accidentally" giving away the hiding place or leaving it around "carelessly." These are signals from the subconscious that *you want it to be found*, for an X-rated reason, even a subconscious ploy to end the relationship. Should this happen, work hard on understanding your motive. You have struck a danger area.

Invent a way to be private without the need to censure, inhibit, disguise, or distort the truth.

We are composed of many parts. The diary is a great way to become acquainted with them. A standard and powerful technique is to write dialogues between two of your selves at a time, and if a third chimes in, it will tell you things in another dimension. For example, if Conscience is fighting Wayward Impulses, try Best Self conversing with Willful Self. If a part of your body is giving you trouble, have Liver tell Head what to do. Perhaps it is being overloaded, and Head may have to call in Glutton for a sounding out. The purpose is twofold: to get information, and to work out a plan for improved action. Emotions and thoughts running riot become manageable when dealt with as *entities* within. Speak to them as such, discover where they come from, what they are trying to do to you, and why. Establish a cooperative effort. At the very least, form a temporary truce.

Dialogue with others can extend to people who are dead, or distant personalities in the public eye. You may love, hate, envy, or use these people as models. If such is the case, hold dialogues with them. If you persist, at some point you will uncover an unresolved part of yourself. Being bonded to someone or something Out There is often a projection of an internal facet of self that has become dissociated and disowned. Projecting someone else's personality onto yourself suggests a part of you that is underdeveloped.

Unsent letters offer another technique. You can write them to strangers, distant friends, or you can compose cool and assertive letters to someone you are living with, filling in voids of communication, trying out different ways to tell them things that have been difficult to verbalize. The things-I-never-told-you letter helps you realize *your* part in the communication block, and prepares you to take responsibility for it.

The letter is a powerful tool that can connect you to your whole range of feelings about someone. The unsent letter is a great catharsis. You can go all the way—even to expressing the wish to murder. Unresolved strong feelings, not acknowledged by the owner, can grow to dangerous intensity. But if they remain on paper, it is most often their final destination.

Ordinarily the diary has one audience—you. In moral confessions, some speak to God. In the diary one can speak to God within, or the real Self, Soul, Hidden or Subliminal Self, as you choose. This is to be kept in mind even if you plan to open your diary, or parts of it, eventually—to friends, family, or the general public. Initially, write for yourself alone without being distracted or inhibited by questions such as: Will they be critical or accepting? Surprised? How would I like them to respond? Can I make it more interesting for them?

Later, you can work on ways to integrate the diary material with your autobiography.

We grew up with literary and philosophical gems like "Know thyself" and "To thine own self be true." Later we realized these were not always easy to accomplish.

Diary writing is a classic, effective method of understanding and changing ourselves. Changing ourselves is one step toward changing the world.

EXERCISE 1. MY WHOLE SELF _____

PURPOSE OF THIS EXERCISE

Diary writing can help you to sort out the segments that compose your personality and to get a perspective on the whole person. This exercise helps to visualize the process.

INSTRUCTIONS

Using the diagram on page 108, select three people with whom you connect in your daily life, or often enough so they affect your life. Mark them by name:

1. (Name) Person #1
2. (Name) Person #2
3. (Name) Person #3

The shaded portions denote the part of the person that overlaps with you. Discuss how this happens—how a part of you is changed, conforms, is deformed, distorted, or enriched by the relationship.

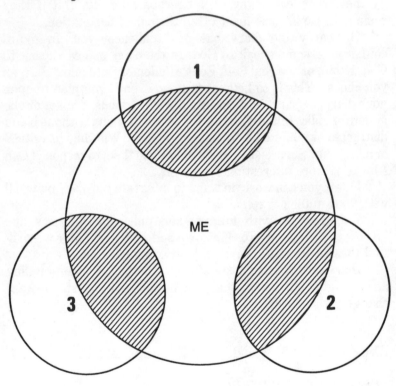

EXAMPLE (A YOUNG DANCER):

Person #1—Ron, my lover. This part represents a quiet spot, a place of emotional rest, but in it are doubts about the rest of me—whether this need for emotional fulfillment depends on him alone so that it will consume and discolor my entire emotional tone, or whether I can leave it contentedly in that small shaded area.

Person #2—Carol, my teacher. She enriches this part of me by forcing me to stretch myself creatively. There is a running battle between my faith in my ability and her faith in me—but the ragged part is gradually healing. This shaded portion, I feel, is spreading to other areas and eventually will help the rest of me gain confidence and grow in general.

Person #3—Sylvia, my cat. She is a pure white, long-haired charmer who is named after an albino girl friend I roomed with at college. I haven't found a girl buddy like that since. Maybe it's because those relationships are more intense in youth, or maybe it's the time—maybe there should still be relationships like that. Sylvia the Cat fills the need for feminine friendship to a degree. She puts demands on a little bit of my time when I come home tired, but she is loving and nurturing too, and worth it.

EXERCISE 2. DEAR SIGNIFICANT OTHER _____

PURPOSE OF THIS EXERCISE
Unsent letters can help fill voids in communication and unblock feelings toward another.

INSTRUCTIONS
Take the most acute communication problem you have at this time. Write a letter to that person. Tell her or him what you have not been able to express face to face. Write your feelings. Write what you would like from the other.

EXAMPLE (A MOTHER TO AN ALCOHOLIC DAUGHTER):

Dear Cindy,

God, I wish I knew the magic words to get through the fixed view you have of me, the view of a small child—Mother will always be there, she'll always put out for me. She's supposed to. When she doesn't, I have a right to get mad.

In Alanon they tell me there's nothing I can do but wait, hope, and pray. Any attempt to help, rescue, or make it easier and softer will only delay the process of your getting sober—if you ever will.

I'm resigned to it, unhappily. It means less contact with you. And no giving, except to keep in touch, to let you know that I still love you, no matter what.

Maybe this unsent letter will loosen up my resistance to telling you these things up front, to find the words, to risk your anger and your pulling away from me. I can't lose you.

I love you so much,
Mom

READINGS

ALCOTT, LOUISA MAY. *Louisa May Alcott, Her Life, Letters, and Journals.* Edited by Edna D. Cheney. Boston: Little, Brown & Co., 1919. The famed author of *Little Women* was her own model for the hard-working Jo.

BALDWIN, CHRISTINA. *One to One.* New York: M. Evans & Co., 1977. A simple discussion of ways to write journals in a free and individual style and for self-understanding.

BASHKIRTSEFF, MARIE. *The Journal of a Young Artist.* Translated by Mary J. Serrano. New York: E. P. Dutton, 1923. Bashkirtseff died at twenty-four, but her diary became famous for its uninhibited show of feelings and fantasies. She was a talented but pampered artist.

FRANK, ANNE. *The Diary of a Young Girl.* Garden City, N.Y.: Doubleday & Co., 1952. Anne's diary was written while in hiding from the Nazis. She was captured and killed. Her story is inspiring because of her marvelous attitude toward life. She wanted to be a writer. She was.

ISHERWOOD, CHRISTOPHER. *Kathleen and Frank.* New York: Simon & Schuster, 1971. One of our finest writers tells about his early life through his mother's diaries, adding his own recollections and comments.

LAGERLÖF, SELMA. *The Diary of Selma Lagerlöf.* Translated by Velma Swanston Howard. Garden City, N.Y.: Doubleday Doran, 1936. Lagerlöf was the first woman to win the Nobel Prize for Literature. This work is noted for its nostalgic and metaphysical experiences.

MANSFIELD, KATHERINE. *The Journal of Katherine Mansfield.* Edited by John Middleton Murray. New York: Alfred A. Knopf, 1927. Mansfield was a woman who defied convention and became a famous short-story writer, using Chekhov as her model. The last part of her life was a struggle with illness.

MOFFAT, MARY JANE, and PAINTER, CHARLOTTE, eds. *Revelations: Diaries of Women.* New York: Random House, 1975. The finest collection of its kind to date, with comments from the authors, both sensitive writers.

NIN, ANAÏS. *The Diary of Anaïs Nin.* 6 vols. Chicago: The Swallow Press, 1966. The books that created a cult of diary writing and study. Read these for study of the detail and devotion that can go into this art form.

PEPYS, SAMUEL. *The Diary of Samuel Pepys.* Los Angeles: University of California Press, 1973. One of the most famous diarists of all time. A remarkable book by a remarkable seventeenth-century man. Sir Arthur Bryant said that "nothing so honest has ever been written by a man of his own self."

PROGOFF, IRA. *At a Journal Workshop.* New York: Dialogue House Library, 1975. Text for the Intensive Journal Workshops. Outlines and explains the process.

SAND, GEORGE. *The Intimate Journal of George Sand.* New York: John Day Co., 1929. The flamboyant writer and adventuress was an incurable romantic and loved to write about it in vivid detail.

SIMONS, GEORGE F. *Keeping Your Journal.* New York: Paulist Press, 1978. Easy-to-read manual on journals with types of books and exercises.

THOREAU, HENRY DAVID. *Walden and Other Writings.* New York: Random House, 1950. The exquisite prose and sensitive insights are as alive today as ever. If you're not familiar with Thoreau, I strongly recommend this as an example of a man who was completely at peace with himself.

TOLSTOY, SOPHIE A. *The Diary of Tolstoy's Wife.* Translated by Alexander Werth. London: Victor Gollancz, 1928. The wife of Leo Tolstoy wrote of her depressions and tempestuous life with the famous writer.

WOOLF, VIRGINIA. *A Writer's Diary.* New York: Harcourt, Brace, 1954
Required reading for anyone interested in raising diary writing to the highest level of the use of language, and in a keen perception of life in general.

8

Words and Psyche

"When I use a word," Humpty Dumpty said,
"it means just what I choose it to mean—
neither more or less."
"The question is," said Alice, "whether
you can make words mean so many different
things."
"The question is," said Humpty Dumpty,
"which is to be the master—that's all."

—LEWIS CARROLL, *Alice in Wonderland*

Autobiography is enriched by special and personal use of language and by understanding the psychology of language. The use of certain words and expressions reflects your response to the world and can influence the way you think, act, and live your life.

Theories of language range from those of "good" or "proper" English to total permissiveness in the way we speak and write. Whichever way you choose is your affair, but keep in mind that the manner should fit the matter. The style, the form, and the content should go together.

To do your book justice, choose the words that project your personality. It's amazing how many people find it hard to write the way they speak. Are you able to come up with just the right word you're looking for, most of the time—the one that will express what you feel or visualize in your mind's eye? Of course, one can be picky to the extreme. Dorothy Parker, the brilliant humorist, once squashed a writer by describing him as the type who "rolls around on the floor for three days looking for a word."

Somerset Maugham shared Parker's feeling in an anecdote about Henry James, the novelist. At a weekend houseparty, the hostess informed James that a young man, another guest, was quite talented. The curious James engaged him in a conversation, and Maugham wrote:

> My friend was petulant and impatient, and at length, driven to desperation by James' interminable struggle to find the one word that would express exactly what he wanted to say, blurted out: "Oh, Mr. James, I'm not of any importance. Don't bother about rooting around for the right word. Any old word is good enough for me."

However, in another essay, Maugham admits that although he thought James obtuse and shallow, "the man was so damned readable!"

The choice of words can make the difference between merely keeping the reader's attention and riveting it so the book can't be put down. A good rule of thumb is that when you can't find the right word, don't impede a writing flow, but "dummy it in," as writers say. It will come to you later, while rolling on the floor or studying a dictionary.

Have a large enough repertoire of words to do the job, but don't get off on a tangent. Studying words is so fascinating that it can consume too much of your writing time and take on too great an importance in relation to other elements of writing.

Here is a simple system to build up a supply of words. There are three vocabularies in your life:

1. The words you know and use. Let's call this one your *usable vocabulary*.

2. The words you recognize and understand when you hear them or read them, but you don't use them. This can be called your *unused vocabulary*.

WORDS AND PSYCHE 115

3. That periphery of words you have encountered but not bothered to look up. You are either not sure of their meaning, have no idea of their meaning, or have never heard them before. This we will call your *mystery vocabulary*.

Start a card-file collection (3 × 5-inch cards will do) with alphabet dividers. As you come across or think of a word you want to use and study, write it on a card. Add sentences you see or hear from time to time containing this word and develop more subtle, finely tuned ways of using it.

To hone your usable vocabulary, give some thought to the words you use now. Study them after you have written something. Use a dictionary of synonyms or a thesaurus. Enter your word on a card, look up synonyms for it, and add to the card. You may even decide you like one of the synonyms better, or you may chuck out some words altogether from your vocabulary. You may get tired of using a certain word, and your friends may get tired of listening to certain repetitive words. Ask them about this and begin polishing your speech patterns.

Important: in collecting words, choose the ones that appeal to your own style and taste. Never mind looking for fancy or acceptable or even "proper" ones. The idea is to build a *personal vocabulary*. The same will be true for expressions and all of your written work. Mainly, allow the readers to meet you, and become their friend.

For your *unused vocabulary*, enter these words gradually on cards as you come across them. If you are ambitious, look them up in *Fowler's Modern English Usage* or any other books on usage that give examples. Copy these examples of sentences on your cards. Some may seem old-fashioned to you. Paraphrase them to suit yourself. Use the words at every opportunity to enrich your speech and writing.

When you encounter *mystery words*, stop and think whether they are ones you wish to add to your collection. Is this word *you?* If so, enter it in your file. Otherwise, just note its meaning for recognition the next time you see or hear it.

Many authors start their writing day by playing with their word collection as a warm-up, adding so many a day to their day's quota of manuscript. Two is a good average. This will give you about 700 extra usable words a year. Most adults don't add more than about twenty a year after they finish school. There is a bonus. Tests have indicated that the I.Q. goes up with the number of words comprehended.

Become aware of the uses of different kinds of words.

Verbs are the most powerful as they connote action. Somebody does something, and your sentence moves. Comb through what you have written and transpose as many nouns, adjectives, and adverbs as possible into active verbs. See if you like what this does for your sentence. Here's an example:

> Nonactive verbs   In *considering* the urgent necessity for a decision *regarding* relocation, there *was* a problem: the 2,000 books in my den.

> VERSUS:

> Active verbs   I *stopped* and *considered* the immediate situation. I *had to move,* and I *had to make* a quick decision. There was a problem: As I *sat* at my desk, I *looked* straight at it: I *faced* a wall of 2,000 books!

In the second version, the reader can visualize the scene more vividly and feel the sense of urgency without being told about it. There are degrees of power in verbs, and this is where word study is so valuable. For example, to say "I procrastinated" is more dynamic than "I kept putting it off." One precise verb in place of several words is usually more readable for its brevity as well as its visual force. There will be times, though, when it will take a few more words to say exactly what you mean.

Nouns establish a base for your visual imagery of "who" or "what." Surround them with descriptions of texture, color, intensity, and feeling. It takes practice to write interesting descriptions. Study the masters such as Somerset Maugham, whose short stories are crammed with superb examples.

Sensual words. Whenever possible, use words which quickly appeal to the senses. *Onomatopoeia* refers to words that sound like what they are describing, such as *hiss, buzz, chatter.* Think of all five senses: sight, sound, taste, smell, and touch. Don't settle for red, green, or blue—in relation to sight-words. Develop nuances as copywriters do to sell clothes and cosmetics: azure, jade, washed in sunlight, aroma of honey-bread baking, scent of lilacs, ice-blue silk caressing fingertips.

Start a romance with words. Fall in love with your favorites.

Bookstores are stuffed with texts on word power and vocabulary building, especially since it was discovered that executives have better vocabularies than worker ants. But don't mix too many systems of word study—it's easy to get confused or blocked. But do get hooked on words. They are the building blocks that will give your book its unique structure.

Writing isn't a science. Teachers and assorted guides vary the ways they arrange the elements of writing under different headings. Some separate the subject of style from grammar and punctuation, others don't. It really doesn't matter, as long as you can wade through theories and find your own way of putting it all together.

The modern trend in writing is shorter sentences, swifter tempo, and the use of fiction techniques in nonfiction. But there are two opposing camps: "modern" versus "traditional," or "colloquial" versus "literary" writing. Colloquial is the popular form used by the media and preferred by many professionals, who insist it is better to write as you talk. It depends on your taste and goal, your mood, and point of time in life. There is nothing wrong with a preference for writing a literary or traditional book. The art of writing is not a thing of the past, as many streamliners of English insist. You can mix literary and popular writing. When you use narration, an artful style is a plus. When writing dialogue, it is more accurate to quote someone in the popular manner—if that is the way the person speaks.

To write convincing dialogue, use one basic and simple principle. Speech cannot be written exactly the way it is spoken or much of it would be unreadable. For example, writing the following sentence phonetically would result in something like this: (the way many, many people speak):

"Whyncha 'av a dip inna swimmy poo', 'n 'en I'll givya bita lunch."

Unless you want to emphasize slovenly speech, you can characterize this person by writing:

"Why don' cha have a dip in the swimming pool, 'n then I'll give you a bite 'v lunch."

A mere suggestion of pop talk will suffice.

In using accents, whether American regional or other nationalities, the solution is to suggest an accent here and there. Thus, "German" dialogue could be written "Ze problem mit living in ze city is too much noise," rather than to try to duplicate every word phonetically.

Everything in writing is permissible, including your use of grammar, punctuation, the way you arrange words into phrases, sentences, and compositions, and the use of pet phrases. Some may want to imitate the style of a favorite author. One student wrote her story in the manner of English women's gothics. This mode gave her story the flavor she was striving for.

Similes stretch the imagination. These are comparisons using "like" or "as": "In the sunlight her hair looked like spun gold." In the *metaphor*, the image is of a substitution rather than comparison: "In the sunlight her hair became spun gold," or "He was her ballast." In the metaphor, one word replaces a whole string of words and says much, making for great economy of word usage and striking images.

Personification gives human qualities to nonhuman things, as in "the angry sea."

For rhythm and sound, *alliteration* can be effective. This is using several words in one sentence beginning with the same letter, for example, "Before drifting off to *sleep*, I imagined I could *see* a *star sailing* through the *sky*." Alliteration is a wonderful way to woo a reader into the mood you wish to create.

Be careful with books about writing style. Most are motivated by personal opinion, some downright prejudiced as if to say: "If you're not doing it my way, you're doing it wrong." Toss out rules that stand in your way. You're aiming at *personalizing* language. You can become so entangled in ponderous approaches on "how-to-do-it" English as to become tongue-tied. Between the "no-nonsense" schools of short sentences, plain words, and no fancy stuff, and the purists who throw a temper tantrum if someone uses a word "improperly," you'll find your own comfortable median of style.

This doesn't mean that you must find one style and stick to it. In autobiography several styles can show different sides to your personality, or growth from one stage to another, or dramatic changes in yourself. Sudden insights release new feelings or intensity of emotions.

We shape our language, but it also shapes us. It shapes us from without (the media, our family, culture, peers, etc.) and from within. You can literally hypnotize yourself with words and expressions and shape your own self-image and behavior. "Why do I always say these stupid things?" if repeated often enough, can make you appear stupid to yourself and to others. "I hate my nose. I've always hated it." (You didn't when you were three months old.) In this way, you can condition yourself to feel ugly. "He drives me crazy" can literally give you hypertension. "She's a pain in the neck," "Get off my back," "This job is a big headache"—expressions such as these can make you develop physical disabilities in your neck, back, and head.

Eric Berne found that when people shifted from one ego state to another, their language changed:

> Typical Parental words are: cute, naughty, low, vulgar, disgusting, ridiculous, and many of their synonyms. Adult words are: unconstructive, apt, parsimonious, desirable Others, expletives and epithets, are usually manifestations of the Child. Substantives and verbs are intrinsically Adult, since they refer without prejudice, distortion, or exaggeration to objective reality.

Gestures, facial expressions, body postures, and voice tones match words. Becoming more aware of this will enrich self-descriptions.

So allow words to flow freely as you write. Later, study which part of you they are coming from. Then, as you describe scenes of the past, you will have more material and understanding to work with. You will have a better vision of yourself in transition—the universal theme in autobiography.

EXERCISE 1. WORD EFFECT_____

PURPOSE OF THIS EXERCISE
    To tighten up, shape up, and if necessary, reshape some of your speech habits.

INSTRUCTIONS
    Devote a day or evening when you are around others. Carry a few 3 × 5 cards.
    Become conscious of repetitive words, phrases, or expressions that you use. Write each on a card.
    Mark down the type of word it is and the effect it has on you emotionally. For example:

1. Qualifies or waters down my statement.

2. Excessive exaggeration.

3. Understatement.

4. Vague, confusing, tentative, uncertain, fuzzy.

5. Reinforces self-esteem.

6. Reinforces lack of self-worth.

7. Absolutes: *never, always, best, worst.*

8. Generalizations: Everybody should exercise. People don't eat enough vegetables.

9. Rubrication (literally, to color it red, meaning a prejudice): Men are little boys. Women are petty. Jews love money.

    Become aware of words or expressions that are overused by you and others because they are "in," such as "fun thing," or "being into" something.
    Give some hard thought to your speech patterns and habits

you want to break. Ask friends to help by pointing these out to you *as they occur,* because they become automatic and we are not often aware of using them.

EXAMPLE (A FASHION DESIGNER, FEMALE):

I became aware that I had a repertoire of catch phrases designed to convince people I was ugly, such as "I'm not bad when I get dressed up," or "He looked at me without screaming." My language revealed I was making jokes out of a very deep, hurtful conviction that I needed a great deal of embellishment to feel O.K. Then it flashed on me why I became a designer!

EXAMPLE (A FILMMAKER, MALE):

I realized that I had an unusually large collection of prejudices and rigidity of perception of people. I connected this to my work, and saw that I photographed people in ways that did not show all sides, literally and figuratively. I now can see room for more freedom in my style of work.

EXERCISE 2. THE EAR AND THE EYE _____

PURPOSE OF THIS EXERCISE

To find your best way of writing and to help you get words on paper. Many people find that when they first start to write, taping their ideas gets them talking like themselves. After a while, they can do either. Many continue to tape. Others loosen up their writing-on-paper skills.

INSTRUCTIONS

Choose an incident you wish to write about, something that will not run more than two written paragraphs, ten to twenty lines.

Tape it (talk into a recorder). Put it away.

The next day (without listening to the tape), write the same incident. Put that away.

On the third day, transcribe the tape. Don't study it yet.

On the fourth day, compare the two written pieces and study them for the following:

Style

Spontaneity

Word usage

Readability

Decide which you liked better. If the taped one, then continue to tape your work. Or use both, combining the best of each.

EXAMPLE (A RETIRED BUSINESSMAN):
I was amazed to discover that I got a kind of stage fright in facing that blank page, and my written language was stilted and not at all like me. When I transcribed the taped material, it sounded like me—although I didn't like the way I talked to everyone, like "the man in charge."

EXAMPLE (A HOUSEWIFE):
Good grief! I seem to be talking a blue streak, much of it just filler and too many excess words. When I tried to write instead, I was inhibited. The way I figure it, is that I mostly talk to children all day, so when I'm with adults, I let it all go out too fast—just the need for conversation! I'm going to have to work on adjusting my writing so that I don't talk to the readers as if they are all children, repeating things needlessly.

EXERCISE 3. WORD ORGY

PURPOSE OF THIS EXERCISE
To learn more words and build a personal collection of words. To make your speech richer in expressing *you.*

INSTRUCTIONS
Choose a few hours or a day when you can be free and undisturbed. This will depend on your mood, receptiveness, stage of progress, and degree of motivation.
Instead of waiting for words to appear for study, take your

dictionary and begin at the beginning, going page by page, reading the words and selecting those that appeal to you. Some may be fancy or unusual. That's O.K. as long as they are those you would like to adopt.

Enter them in your card file.

Quit this session when you are satiated.

Do it again when you are ready to absorb more.

COMMENTS ON RESULTS

EXAMPLE (A LAW STUDENT):

I found it hard to get my head into learning too many new words—I'm having to memorize a lot of legal terms. But I also found out that my general vocabulary is pretty thin, and I'd better learn to talk better if I want to perform in a courtroom.

EXAMPLE (A RETIRED WIDOW):

It's too hard at my age to change my habits. Maybe if I could do it slowly . . . I did find some words that I liked and never used, and I was surprised that I caught the gist of so many words I've never actually used.

EXAMPLE (AN ACTOR):

I love words, so the trouble is that I could easily get sidetracked. I could spend a whole weekend doing nothing but making lists of words I want to integrate into my daily speech, and many more I would like to use in my writing.

EXERCISE 4. DESCRIPTIONS_____

PURPOSE OF THIS EXERCISE

One way to develop style is to write short descriptions. There are two steps, done at different times.

INSTRUCTIONS

1. Choose a quiet time when you are alone in a familiar room. Study your surroundings with a fresh eye—your writer's eye—as if you were someone seeing it for the first time. Use the third-person, objective point of view.

Write a paragraph on a 3 × 5 card, describing a few things

in the room. Add a few comments about the kind of person you think inhabits this room.

2. Using the first-person, subjective point of view, choose a time when other people are with you. Pick one of these people. Whip out a 3 × 5 card and write a few sentences containing:

Why he or she is in that room.

How he or she looks and sounds in relation to the others.

The mood or feeling in the room.

What happened in this scene? Treat the scene like a ministory: people came together, something is happening, a conclusion.

You can substitute a scene from memory if it is not convenient to write it this way.

EXAMPLES

Third-person point of view (a man's den): It was a mishmash of a room. Institutional gray walls, bare window, bruised carpet—all against lush plants wherever a space would hold one. The organized clutter on the desk and the unused lounging chair (piled with books and manuscripts) gave the message that here was a man with no time for the frills of living.

Third-person point of view (a model's bedroom): The bed, draped in a pink rose pattern, was angled in the center of the room and she could not tell which way the girl slept on it. A hill of pillows was piled in the center. The same rose pattern on the drapes, the round tables and chaise, gave the effect—well, let's be honest—like the rest of her trappings, they were for effect.

First-person point of view (living room in home of older woman active in the community): Eight or nine of us clustered around the canapes. Rona looked on quietly, and only I knew she was there to "make contacts." On the periphery of the festive mood of the group, she had a way of looking up at people as if she were looking down at them.

It was all in the sharp brown-black eyes, loose long jet hair, and flowing clothes. This night she had costumed herself as a lady of mystery, seldom uttering a sound. When she did, there was a soft, menacing gothic hiss between the words.

First-person point of view (a house in Hollywood shared by two women painters): People arrived in a steady stream from eight o'clock on, carrying mounds of food on exotic trays and hand-crafted bowls. Peg worked the hostess role to the hilt, determined that everyone should have a great time (good wasn't good enough) if she had to shake heaven and earth. Her tie-dyed chiffon caftan in cool sea shades blended with the 9 × 12 wall hanging up for sale. This was the third night in a row she demanded I be charming to everyone until four A.M. On that night I knew I lacked the quantity and quality of charm required to be Peg's roommate.

READINGS

CHASE, STUART. *The Tyranny of Words.* New York: Harcourt, Brace & Co., 1938. General semantics, the theory of the meaning and effect of words and language in general.

EHRLICH, IDA. *Instant Vocabulary.* New York: Pocket Books, 1969. A comprehensive workbook for building vocabulary.

FLESCH, RUDOLF. *The Art of Plain Talk.* New York: Harper & Bros., 1946. One of the best basic books on the use of popular language.

FUNK, WILFRED, and LEWIS, NORMAN. *30 Days to a More Powerful Vocabulary.* New York: Pocket Books, 1945. A powerful little book that has text and exercises by the famous team, authors of books on writing.

MENCKEN, H. L. *The American Language.* New York: Alfred A. Knopf, 1947. The fundamental text of formal or "proper" English for those who wish to learn the fine-tunings of the language and subtle meanings and differences among words.

STRUNK, WILLIAM, JR., and WHITE, E. B. *The Elements of Style.* New York: The Macmillan Co., 1959. A little book that has been treasured for years by students of the language as a basic guide to good form and crisp, uncluttered writing style.

9

Getting It Down on Paper

*You cannot write well
unless you write much.*

—SOMERSET MAUGHAM

All your good intentions, attendance at classes and conferences, book collections, and even determination won't guarantee that you will cross over into that charmed dimension where you will perform the act of writing.

It can only be done by those who understand and accept what they are in for, and persist.

Too many projects peter out because a writer got stuck or discouraged or confused—and quit as a result. An amazing number of books on writing are discouraging. They give the impression that everything can be taught—except writing. Authorities too often talk down to the "novice," "aspirant," "writer-in-training," or downright "amateur," warning about the greats with whom they will be competing, spreading gloom about the hazards of the trade.

Dorothea Brande says, in *Becoming a Writer:*

> The reasons for this pessimism about young writers are dark to me. Books written for painters do not imply that the chances are that the reader can never be anything but a conceited dauber.

126

It takes a few simple steps to succeed. I said simple—not easy. First, know that you *can* do it. Then dispense with myths about writing, writers, and the writer's life. Approach this task as you would if you were setting out to learn welding or water-skiing. Be prepared to give it conscientious, persistent application.

Above all, you'll need patience and the willingness to spend a lot of time alone with yourself.

Telling someone to face a blank page without any guidance on how to begin is like asking someone who can't swim to learn by jumping into the deep end of a pool and "simply" start thrashing around.

Here arc a few common mistaken beliefs about writing, in italics, followed by my comments:

1. *Grab a pencil, apply the seat of your pants to the seat of the chair, and just start.* Writing craft has procedures and principles. Skill is developed by work. However, it is not a field for weaklings.

2. *There are writers and the rest of us, or You either got it or you ain't.* True, some people have what seems a way with words, but it would not have developed if they hadn't worked at it.

3. *Writing can't be taught.* There is both a craft and an art to writing. The craft or mechanics can and are being taught successfully. Art is developed by inviting intuition and a transcendent view of reality—a personal way of seeing things. Both will blossom with regular, applied effort.

4. *Writing has to be painful.* It is for some, not for others. You can train yourself to enjoy it.

5. *A writer should be able to dash off material in odd moments, or to write anywhere.* Not so. Writing habits are personal. Do it any way that leads to productivity.

6. *A writer should wait for inspiration.* It has also been said that good writing is ten percent inspiration and ninety percent perspiration.

7. *If you haven't written by the time you are forty, you never will. Or, if you're young, you don't have anything really important to say.* Age doesn't matter, but whenever you begin, prepare to put in an apprenticeship.

In short, take a fresh view of the writing field.

You now fit into one of these broad categories: you work full time and must moonlight your writing; you work part time and can write part time; you can devote full time to it.

There are tough teachers who say that if you are serious, you'll find time right now. But to be realistic, you may need to change your job or your life-style to find that time.

For example, after much intimidation by the "seat-of-the-pants" theory, I had to give up school for a summer and stretch out my course load in order to complete a writing project.

Another example is one student had to change jobs, to one less taxing on her creative energy, and the writing began to flow just as she was ready to give up.

Don't torture yourself with unrealistic goals. Keep chopping away until you hit on a plan that works. Don't always blame yourself if it doesn't. Just keep chopping.

Experiment with *time*. Many full-time writers find the morning hours most conducive to creative work. A classic example was Somerset Maugham, who wrote from about 9 A.M. until about 1 P.M., seven days a week. After lunch he socialized. Evenings, regardless of the glitter of an event, he excused himself at about 10 P.M. and retired, so he could rise early.

Irving Wallace finds that he does his best writing *after* an evening's socializing, continuing through early morning and rising late.

Moss Hart, in his story, "Act One," says he could do his writing on and off at will—catching minutes in taxis, or sitting for hours in a quiet spot underneath the boardwalk when he was young and enthusiastic.

Place is highly individual. The time-honored attic has almost disappeared, but most writers prefer a place where they can't be interrupted. Virginia Woolf insisted that if women are to write well, they must have a room of their own—and a fixed income. Well, Virginia, what if we don't? Many busy mothers use libraries or park benches. If you can't do it while stirring the soup, that doesn't mean you're not a writer.

However, homemakers often block themselves by assuming they must do everything for their families. They continue to feed their little boy even if he's forty-five years old. A five-year-old can learn to make a sandwich or warm the soup. The overprotective attitude of the homemaker cripples the self-reliance of her family and her own creative energy.

Some writers are stimulated by the passing crowd and like to face a window on a busy scene. Others work best facing a blank wall. Some like background noise or play records, others carry ear-stoppers wherever they go.

Lucky or ingenious writers find fairer climes. Hemingway loved Spain, F. Scott Fitzgerald adopted Paris, Henry James preferred to associate with the British, Maugham was inspired by the Pacific islands.

A study of how writers work revealed that certain general life-styles go with the territory: "In New York writers commute; in Hollywood they swim; in Paris argue; in Dublin starve."

Writers usually have specific preferences for writing materials: longhand versus typing; the beat-up old standard versus the newest noiseless, self-erasing, electric typewriter; pencils or pens from fine to heavy; green ink or purple paper. Tools and toys are part of the fun.

An actor friend studied up on the accoutrements of writers and became so enchanted with the image of being one that he dusted off an old typewriter, bought a pipe with an assortment of tobacco, retrieved an old sweater from the Goodwill sack, bought reams of twenty-pound bond paper, a dozen Blackwing pencils—and sat for weeks staring at a blank page. The only thing missing was a cat, but only because his wife was allergic to them. I assured him a cat wouldn't do it. What does is beginning to get words on paper, and the more words, the closer you are to being a writer.

So if you can write best while doing a yoga headstand in lotus position, don't let anyone tell you you're crazy.

Read books by writers whose work stimulates your writing flow. And cold as it seems, be aware of which friends stimulate or stifle the flow. People sometimes treat writers strangely, and unwittingly sabotage their efforts. Your effort to write has powerful competition for your time: friends, family, the media (television, radio, magazines, newspapers), pets, home, possessions needing repair, salespeople, compulsive eating, drinking, insomnia, anxiety and stress, pills that dull the thought processes, the telephone, small talk, technology, and temptations. We live in a world of distractions. If they aren't there, we pursue them.

Many writers will do anything to keep from writing—endless trips to the bathroom, water cooler, or refrigerator—with every known excuse. They are very imaginative when it comes to goofing off. There are cures for this.

Desire to write is not enough. You have to progress to the state of *decision*. Give this some hard thought. Have you really made the decision to write? If so, it's still not enough. Decision may get you going but not keep you going. It takes *determination*—solidly establishing the habit. One way is through behavior-modification techniques. This uses your machine part, the part that deals with data gathering and skill development. I don't believe that "man is just a machine," but your computer part can be programmed to do almost anything.

Your goal is a desired behavior, in this case, to write regularly. The principle involved is that the desired behavior will be evoked by *a reward given immediately after it is performed.*

It's the way dolphins and other animals are trained. The trainer waits for the dolphin to perform an action, then a reward is given immediately. Automatically, in time, the dolphin will perform on cue, knowing a reward is waiting. A live fish may be a reward to a dolphin, but you must decide what is a reward to you. Then the process begins.

1. Make a list of activities, food, etc., that are pleasurable to you. At this point, do not apply moral judgments as to whether these things are good for you, self-indulgent, time-wasting, or whatever. Allow yourself anything you like—without guilt. It's that simple.

2. Now make a work schedule, using those hours you know you can count on. Allow for realistic breaks—these will be the times for rewards. Remember: break *plus* reward.

3. Add to the schedule *specific* items from your reward list, writing them down exactly as you will do them. Make it a daily schedule, deciding in the morning or the night before exactly when the break times will occur, and the reward in each. For example:

> 9:00–11:00   Write
> 11:00–11:30   Cup of coffee and crossword puzzle

4. *Important:* After a few days, if you find that the schedule isn't working too well, change it. If your schedule is to write from 9:00 to 11:00 and you find yourself beginning about 10:30, *change the schedule* to 10:30–12:30, or whatever.

If you find that you do better by taking ten-minute breaks every hour instead of half-hour breaks every two hours, revise that. We all have different rhythms. Mold your own realistic schedule—but once a schedule works out with some feeling of comfort, hold to it until you have mastered it.

Find the healthy line between unrealistic rigidity and self-indulgence.

Do not eliminate the rewards at any time. They are the key to the retraining. In time you will know when it is safe to drop them—or if you want to. The important thing at this stage is to set out to do something, and do it. The subconscious will take over, and the desired behavior will become automatic and easy. Writing may even become its own reward.

In spite of all your good intentions and determination, there may be times when nothing will happen. Where there was discouragement, there is now frustration. Perhaps you have made an abortive beginning, perhaps several.

All writers have these dry spells. You'll hear the term "writer's block." It is actually a "living block," but has varied and multiple causes.

Check out your physical state. Are you taking "just an occasional" tranquilizer or sleeping pill? These have an accumulative effect, and sooner or later it catches up with you, attacking your creative energy, dulling it, distorting it. How is your diet? Too much refined carbohydrate, junk foods, sugar, and not enough vegetables and fruits, raw and cooked, will diminish your energy. This, too, has an accumulative effect (especially the buildup of chemicals in processed foods), and within your total energy range is that precious psychic element, *initiative*.

If it's not a physical problem, there may be a psychological problem, unsolved, unfaced, siphoning off creativity. Face that problem to free your creativity.

Technology is a monster attacking our personal progress, hampering our growth. One day the roof leaks; and as soon as that's fixed, the car breaks down; and when that's fixed, the roof starts leaking again. Things break down more often than they used to and don't stay fixed because of poor workmanship and slapdash service, absence of the old-time pride of workmanship. The antidote is to simplify life as much as you can—fewer possessions, and regular times set aside for tending them. Never mind what the Joneses are up to. Have *they* written any good books?

The deadliest enemy of all is our bag of misconceptions. Nothing destroys the writing process more than outdated or handed-down falsehoods about writing.

For example, relying on the judgment of friends and family as to the value of your project can stop you before you begin. They are not your average readers—to *you*, that is. "Readers are only interested in important people." "Publishers are only interested in celebrities." "You write such great letters, you don't need more writing lessons." Or they start to pick your ideas to pieces. How do you feel after they've given you their critique? If it doesn't energize you, something is wrong with the critique, not with you. It's safest not to show your work to anyone except a teacher or workshop colleague. Accept constructive criticism only, and beware of people who tear your effort apart and don't help you put it back together. "The whole middle part needs fixing." (Why? How?) "I'd throw out chapters two and three and put in something more interesting." (Like what?)

A fast first sale can be as traumatic as a first rejection slip. One top editor said that only one percent of writers who submit and sell their first work ever submit again! Riding on an easy success can stifle the hard work necessary for ongoing productivity.

Rejection slips can be regarded as proof of work, and as stepping-stones to improvement. Make the most of them by yanking information out of agents and editors as to why your piece fell short. If the same reason shows up regularly, it may indicate a habit that needs to be corrected. There's an old saying, "You're not a writer until you have papered a wall with rejection slips." Even the top writers don't sell everything they write.

Impatience can lead to discouragement. Trying for a top market too soon, before your work is ready for the "slicks," blurs your perspective on building toward finished work.

Create your own techniques for breaking blocks. Never mind how weird they seem. Ernest Hemingway defrosted the refrigerator. Art Buchwald doesn't like suffering alone, so he bothers everyone else. Barbara Tuchman nurtures herself with a new dress or a chocolate soda. Others stay with it, glued to the typewriter, sweating it out.

The craft of writing is personal, but all writers share the common task of having to turn out many words, as a gymnast expects to do thousands of turns before getting one right.

EXERCISE 1. REVVING UP TO WRITE _____

PURPOSE OF THIS EXERCISE

To begin to collect anecdotes, comments, opinions, and reactions to things that have strong meaning for you.

This is the kind of material that makes the best stories and will help you get in touch with what things provoke the most powerful emotions in you. A pattern may emerge.

When you have enough cards, or when they become unmanageable, begin to label them, and file them in an index system of your own, just so that you can find them when you want them. They will come in very handy to spice up your story.

INSTRUCTIONS

Always carry a bunch of 3 × 5 cards in your pocket or handbag. Whenever you feel a strong reaction to something, jot it down, even if it's just an expletive.

EXAMPLES

1. I got a sudden hard knot in my solar plexis when I saw Matilda at the funeral. She hadn't been to see Ronnie when she was alive and not well, only when Ronnie invited the family to those big dinners. Well, I guess that's one of the things to expect at a funeral. But damn it, why did it bother me that much? It didn't seem to bother Ronnie's children. In fact, they seemed happy to have Matilda, the celebrity, there.

2. The car swerved in front of me so fast I was scared out of my wits. I had the feeling that this total stranger was out to get me because I hadn't changed lanes fast enough to suit him, or whatever the hell it was all about. There are so many nuts on the freeway. It dredged up that periodic longing to get out of this rotten town. But how?

EXERCISE 2. TALK BACK ⎯⎯⎯⎯⎯⎯⎯⎯⎯⎯⎯⎯⎯

PURPOSE OF THIS EXERCISE

Using the same system as in Exercise 1, talk back to the TV or radio—out loud—whenever you have a strong reaction to something you hear. Record your comments and file them.

Note: Much terrific material can be gathered by carrying around a tape recorder while you are driving or walking. Concentrate on the driving or walking—and what you record will be under the edge of consciousness—free and intuitive.

EXERCISE 3. MECHANICAL WRITING ⎯⎯⎯⎯⎯⎯⎯⎯⎯

PURPOSE OF THIS EXERCISE

Getting used to the pure mechanical act of writing—putting pen to paper and turning out words.

INSTRUCTIONS

Keep a pad at your bedside. The moment you awake, write a few sentences, anything that comes to mind.

If nothing comes to mind, write that: "Nothing comes to mind, but I will do this every morning just to warm up my fingers flowing on a piece of paper."

READINGS

BRANDE, DOROTHEA. *Becoming a Writer.* New York: Harcourt, Brace and Co., 1934. A gem of a book that is truly inspiring to beginning writers. Discusses the subtle process of the art and craft and the writer's life.

COWLEY, MALCOLM, ed. *Writers at Work.* New York: The Viking Press, 1958. An ongoing series of interviews with famous writers and the ways they work. From the *Paris Review.*

MAUGHAM, W. SOMERSET. *A Writer's Notebook.* Garden City, N.Y.: Doubleday & Co., 1953. Jottings and recollections, scraps of descriptions, and other raw material collected for future writing. Shows how one great writer achieves part of his richness of language and ideas.

TRIMBLE, JOHN R. *Writing with Style.* Englewood Cliffs, N.J.: Prentice-Hall, 1975. A small text, packed with details and instructional guides to the writing process. For those who want to work at serious writing.

ZIEGLER, ISABELLE. *The Creative Writer's Handbook.* New York: Barnes & Noble, 1975. A dandy little book by an outstanding college teacher. For those willing and able to work hard.

10

Nonfiction

It all belongs to you, the good and the bad, the ecstasy, the remorse and sorrow, the people and the places and how the weather was. If you can get so that you can give that to people, then you are a writer.

—ERNEST HEMINGWAY

Reality and illusion merge and emerge in mysterious rhythm as the autobiographer reenters the past. Fact and fiction will blend. Most autobiographies are written as nonfiction, but there are similarities between nonfiction and fiction: scenes, descriptions, statements, suspense, dialogue. There are mechanics to conquer in craft—structure, unity, and clarity—and every story, true or false, needs a beginning, a middle, and an ending.

One difference between nonfiction and fiction is that autobiography ought to sound like *you.* The style can be more natural than literary styles of fiction, but there is no rule against writing a stylized factual book—and still being you.

The advantage in writing your story in nonfiction form, especially if it is your first book, is that you start with a ready-made protagonist, a cast of characters, and a story line. You have a wide variety of choice in organization. You can probe deeply into a major theme of your life, or you can arrange the many stories that comprise your life as an odyssey or a plot with subplots.

If you're writing to sell, you'll be happy to know that nonfiction outsells fiction and is easier to sell. Fiction may bring greater profits at first, but nonfiction has a longer life span.

Don't feel that you're settling for less if you choose nonfiction as your story's form. This form has literary stature, and its power, especially in the autobiography, is that it's rooted in historical fact. People are fascinated and moved by true stories.

A book is a big job, and the story of your life is a big subject for you. If the vision of the massive job of writing a book intimidates you, start with a short piece as a warm-up. Write about one event, one opinion, one area of expertise. Then, to keep from being overwhelmed, break the book into possible workable parts.

Think through the basics of organization and ingredients, and make specific decisions before you begin to do the actual writing. Bits and pieces can be written as they come to you—scenes, descriptions, opinions, interesting phrases or expressions. At least make notes, or things will slip away.

When you actually start writing, your wealth of experience can be expressed in countless ways through selection, interpretation, and by your style of commentary.

You have a rainbow of personalities to work with: the self you know, the self you don't know, your past and present selves in relation to each other, and the many selves others know. What you don't know when you begin, you'll discover as you write. As material appears, you may need to revise your basic plan, perhaps a number of times. The central challenge of autobiography is the interplay between the events of your life and your memory, perception, and attitude toward them—an exciting cat-and-mouse game between your mind and psyche. As your life reopens itself to you and you record it, you will create a self-portrait in words. The first decision, then, is which self-image to project.

Don't think of this as the only book you'll ever write. It gives an inhibiting finality to whatever you will do. Many people write a series of self-stories, as did Eleanor Roosevelt, Simone de Beauvior, and Jean-Paul Sartre. Why not you? Start with the one you're burning to write *now.* Determine the tone of your book and the psychological place you're coming from. Which personality will be featured? What is the main reason for writing it? For example:

To present your life just as a series of free-flowing happenings. (Tone: breezy, light.)

To be a model for a way of life or philosophy. (Tone: moral, but just slightly, please.)

To influence or persuade. (Tone: charismatic.)

To show how your life was shaped by a special theory about behavior. (Tone: pedagogic, but subtle.)

To show your passion for an art, occupation, place, or lifestyle. (Tone: enthusiastic, emotional.)

To present yourself as self-confident, an integrated personality, and how you achieved this state. (Tone: positive, adult.)

To present yourself in conflict, still struggling to work things out. (Tone: human, open, natural, forming goals and getting there.)

To unburden yourself. (Tone: tempestuous.)

Even though you are writing the book primarily for yourself, your attitude toward the reader is part of your world attitude. Think about these suggestions:

Avoid sounding as if you were talking down to the reader. Talk straight.

Avoid sounding perfect. There's a saying, "If you think you're perfect, no one can stand you; if you don't think so, you can't stand yourself."

Avoid sounding too mixed up or miserable. The reader may think, "I'm mixed up, the writer's mixed up, too. What good does this do me?"

There are three basic types of books on the market today: those that inform, those that entertain, and those that stimulate emotionally. Autobiography can fit these categories.

The informational type has enough interesting facts or new ideas to justify a book. If it's not strong enough or deep enough, don't waste it—turn it into an article.

In the entertainment type, the subject is less important than how you tell it. The subject is usually light, but can have subtle undertones of meaning. This type is generally about something especially interesting, unusual, or funny. To make this type of book work, spice it with sharp dialogue, insight into human feelings and foibles, descriptive detail, and humor. Sometimes humor is the only thing that helps us cope. For example, Erma Bombeck's hilarious comments on everyday life help us laugh together at some of the craziness we encounter in today's world.

To stimulate and arouse emotion, a connective link is made between yourself and the reader. The craft problem here is whether this link can be sustained through a whole book. If so, it needs to be varied at intervals. If it's a heavy subject, it will need to be relieved by humor, light comments, changes of scene or tack.

You have thought about the general purpose of your book, your self-image, and the category or type. Now decide which form will best contain your material. Keep in mind that these forms are not rigid or static. They usually overlap, as you will see. It's a matter of emphasis.

TYPES OF NONFICTION

JOURNALS, LETTERS, AND OTHER MEMORABILIA

Many students who come to autobiography workshops have been keeping journals for years. Some feel a psychic overload as they face this mountain of material, often not organized. If this is a problem to you, sort it through with the techniques suggested in Chapter 5 on harvesting historical data. After the material is organized in volumes, distill these into *one volume.* When this is done, you'll have a clearer perspective on your internal history.

THE CHRONOLOGICAL OR PANORAMIC AUTOBIOGRAPHY

This is your complete story from birth to the present. It is mostly used by those who want to reconstruct as much of their lives as possible. An *unabridged version* includes diaries, letters, photographs, invitations, announcements, newspaper items—everything you have hung onto. One student even saved her grocery lists. It's a personal archive to go to for information or pleasure. You can make an abridged copy in which you select parts of your life, capturing the events of your life in an even flow. But it is still a record.

THE LIFE REVIEW

This is a slightly different chronological record, an abridged version. You select and write about the significant patterns unique to your life. Outer life is seen in counterpoint to inner life, and how it fashioned your personality. This type of autobiography is very popular with older people who want to coordinate their thoughts about the way they lived, how they feel about each part of their lives, and their lives as a whole. The main idea is to face *all* of it, survey it, analyze it, accept it, and feel all right about it. A life review can be done for yourself alone or to hand down to your family as a heritage and to help them understand you better.

Benjamin Franklin's autobiography is a kind of life review, addressed to his son, in the form of a letter:

> *Dear Son:*
>
> *I have ever had pleasure in obtaining any little anecdotes of my ancestors. You may remember the inquiries I made among the remains of my relations when you were with me in England, and the journey I undertook for that purpose. Imagining it may be equally agreeable to you to know the circumstances of my life, many of which you are not yet acquainted with. . . .*

Franklin said he sat down to write "expecting the enjoyment of a week's uninterrupted leisure"! For this remarkable feat he had to be extremely well organized. I can't improve on his system. It was so simple. First, he made an outline which he called his Draft Scheme, in staccato sentences, beginning as follows:

> My writing. Mrs. Dogood's letters. Differences arise between my Brother and me (his temper and mine); their cause in general. His Newspaper. The Prosecution he suffered. . . .

He then wrote his story as it flowed from his pen, interspersed with comments and bits of philosophy. If he rambled, well, then, he rambled and accepted himself graciously, pausing to observe himself:

> By my rambling digressions I perceive myself to be growing old. I us'd to write more methodically. But one does not dress for private company as for a publick hall. 'Tis perhaps only negligence.

THE PARTIAL AUTOBIOGRAPHY

John Dean introduces his book *Blind Ambition* with a clear statement about the type of book it is:

> This book is a portrait, not a black and white photograph, of five years of my life. It represents my best effort to paint what I saw and reproduce what I heard. I've included detail, texture, tone, to make this history more vivid, though I trust no prettier.

I call this type of autobiography partial because it is primarily about a specific period of a life and a significant episode contained by it—but it is also a portrait.

THE THEMATIC AUTOBIOGRAPHY

This can cover a lifetime or feature the theme of a part of your life. An example is the classic *Zen in the Art of Archery* by Eugen Herrigal. Though it describes a period of Herrigal's life in a Buddhist monastery (partial autobiography), the theme is his search for a deeper understanding of the nature of life, a search begun before the period described. Again, it is a matter of emphasis. Thematic stories have a specific point of view, a statement to make. Gandhi's *An Autobiography* expresses the important point in his subtitle, *The Story of My Experiments with Truth.* He carries this theme through the story as his life's quest, connecting it to everything that happened to him and everything he made happen.

THE MEMOIR

This form spotlights the *other person,* event, or place, but you are the one casting the light with your thoughts and feelings about it. Your role is observer, narrator, and commentator. An outstanding example is Mary McCarthy's *Memories of a Catholic Girlhood,* in which she describes convent life and her struggles with theology—through her feelings, wrestling with independent thought when she was a young girl.

THE PORTRAIT

This presents someone you knew and think well enough of to fill a book. A much-loved portrait is *My Gandhi* by John Haynes Holmes, whose life was changed by his friendship with Gandhi. Though it's a deeply emotional book about his feelings toward the man, the center of stage is given to Gandhi—his personality, character, dreams, and goals.

THE REMINISCENCE, RECOLLECTION, MEDITATION, OR REVERIE

This form features your feeling side. It goes far back in history. Marcus Aurelius, the second-century philosopher-emperor, is said to have written his famous *Meditations* in moments between affairs of state and on the eve of crucial battles, which explains their fragmented form. Form is less important than *what* you have to say. C. G. Jung's autobiography, *Memories, Dreams, and Reflections,* is a chronological autobiography (with scientific and philosophical digressions), but the key to Jung's personality was his lifelong, deeply reflective nature. He opens with, "My life is a story of the self-realization of the unconscious," and he refers to this book as "telling stories."

THE CONFESSION

The confession is a longtime favorite. The first famous work by Saint Augustine was analytical and cathartic. His book, and books by later writers, cleared the way for the confession's acceptability and popularity. Jean-Jacques Rousseau's classic *Confessions* is not apologetic or contrite, but a search for the true self and a statement about the elusiveness of that self. Thomas De Quincey, in *Confessions of an English Opium Eater*, used his experiences with the drug "to emblazon the power of opium," but he also wrote about opium as a symbol to reflect on human consciousness. The confession is a powerful form, if the positive result is featured. Modern confessions are usually descriptions of how one "came to realize" a truth or changed from "bad" to "good," and how it happened.

Even if a book is your main objective, articles can be by-products. They can absorb material that doesn't fit the story or would clutter it. Nothing need be wasted.

Articles can be about almost anything, but there are general categories found in most magazines:

> *Opinion articles.* Should be backed up by factual material. This type will have to compete with a barrage of opinion articles by authority figures with prestigious positions and credentials. But if you have something special to offer, don't be intimidated.

> *Educational articles.* Offer an experience or skill useful or interesting to others. But personalize it so it doesn't read like something available in an encyclopedia.

> *Amusement or entertainment article.* These are well liked for relaxation and escape value. You can share your experiences of interesting people, places, organizations, unusual things someone you knew did or you did yourself, or just a comment about the human condition.

Another category is by type of article:

THE HOW-TO ARTICLE

This most popular type tells how to become more happy, rich, popular, sexy, or spiritual. People are fanatically curious about how other people do things. Americans have a passion for self-improvement. There are two general types. The *how-to-do-it* article gives specific directions for making or doing something to improve one's social, psychological, or economic state, to learn or sharpen a skill. There are two rules for this one: (1) Directions must be clear enough for the average person to follow. (2) The project must work. Don't offer it unless you have actually done it yourself. Your cake didn't fall, and your brass-and-glass table didn't wobble. Magazines are strict about this. If readers send angry letters because the project cost them time and money, expect an angry letter from the publisher.

The second type is the *how-it-is-done* article. If, for example, you own and operate a sweater-dyeing plant, or test people for vocational skills, there are thousands out there curious to know how these things are done. This type of article reads like a "story behind the news." Everyone knows that sweaters get dyed and vocational tests are administered, but few ever lose that childhood inquisitiveness about how things work.

THE SHORT PORTRAIT OR CHARACTER STUDY

This type is about an unusual person, or anyone who did an unusual thing, and is described *through the actions of the person*. Use anecdotes to demonstrate why you admire the person so that the reader can see what you saw and feel what you felt. The emphasis is on human behavior. Personalize it, explaining your connection to the person, the activity, or the philosophy.

THE TRAVEL ARTICLE

Whatever else you write will be in a setting. It's important to project the feeling of that place into your writing. Writing a travel article helps develop this skill, especially for writing books. The travelog is a time-honored kind of writing always in demand. People are restless, curious, and too often dream of ' greener grass." In John Steinbeck's book *Travels With Charley* (subtitled *In Search of America*), he says that when people heard of his plan to travel for a year through the country:

> ... neighbors came to visit, some neighbors we didn't even know we had. I saw in their eyes something I was to see over and over in every part of the nation—a burning desire to go, to move, to get under way, anyplace, away from the Here.

Wanderlust is semisatisfied for armchair travelers by particular ingredients in travel articles, and these haven't changed much through the years.

1. Choose an aspect of the trip. Don't tell everything that happened to you as you would in a personal log.

2. Use subject matter that is unusual, something they won't find in a travel guidebook. John Steinbeck was the first to travel across the country in a specially built truck with a "house" on it (named Rocinante after Don Quixote's horse) and a poodle named Charley as sole companion. But even if you traveled in an ordinary automobile, you have made a discovery of something different off the beaten track, or have had a special personal experience such as revisiting a childhood scene. You can describe it the way it looked twenty years ago.

3. Use descriptive detail. Unless you have total recall, use the standard technique for travel articles: take all the color photos you can, including closeups. Later you can study them and describe the details you missed.

4. Flowery terms are tempting, especially if you have been moved by a breathtaking scene, but avoid cliches like "pebbles shone like diamonds on the velvet shoreline." Find your own natural way of describing what you saw. If it comes in lyrical terms, I don't want to inhibit you, but it is easy to get carried away by expressions that have been overused.

5. Be sure of your facts. Check out names, addresses, and all detailed data and record them as you go, keeping an orderly log.

6. Integrate comments when you can so as not to stop the visual flow. An example from Steinbeck:

(A woody hill) The top is shaved off and a television relay station lunges at the sky and feeds a nervous picture to thousands of tiny houses clustered like aphids beside the roads.

THE INFORMAL ESSAY

This form of nonfiction states an opinion and proves it, or at least defends a point of view skillfully. It doesn't have to be about a technical or complex issue. You can develop a point of view about everyday things such as food, walking, running, being a good listener, the art of friendship, how it feels to watch your kittens playing.

Before you prepare an article for a magazine, check out the subject in *The Reader's Guide to Periodical Literature* at your library. Make sure that magazine didn't publish anything close to your idea within the last year, or that you have a fresh slant on the idea.

CRAFT IN NONFICTION

There is no formal system of craft. You'll see that books on writing vary, from the laying down of strict rules to the assertion by a prominent playwright who said, "Form and technique are nonsense." But there are some things that appear over and over in books and in interviews with writers when they are pressed to talk about what they do, how they do it, and what they learned.

THE IDEA, THEME, STATEMENT

Books on writing dwell at great length on the problem of how to get ideas. But you already have your basic idea—*you*. Your idea problem is what and how to tell about yourself. An idea is a story in miniature. For example:

> After changing professions three times and beginning to feel himself a failure, a forty-five-year-old single father finds his true vocation and feels at peace for the first time.

The theme is the moral or truth beneath the story. Using the above idea, the theme could be:

A man can be lured into providing a high standard of living for his family by taking a well-paying job he hates, and being forced to give up his earlier dreams.

A statement is just what it says. Tell something the way you see it. For example:

Don't marry too soon, or marry a woman who is willing to struggle if necessary, and wait to have children, so that a man with a dream can realize it.

Select one dominant thread as a story. Try to state it in one sentence. Be sure you know exactly what you want to say before you develop it. If you try to put too many ideas together, the threads will tangle.

You'll encounter differences of opinion about what makes an idea important, especially the general male and female point of view. Women are often told their ideas are too "thin." A generation ago, it was assumed that topics interesting to women were minor, such as flower shows and gossip. This notion has not been erased altogether. In spite of changing male and female stereotyped images, men still have trouble handling emotion, domestic problems, and intimacy, in both life and literature. Unless the hero in a story kills an alligator or parachutes into active enemy bush, the story supposedly carries no weight. Here are some twentieth-, not eighteenth- or nineteenth-, century quotes:

I like writing about beautiful women, and I like putting them in exotic locations. If I wrote a novel about a Kansas farmhouse and a family with problems it would bore not only the reader but myself. (A famous screenwriter)

Most writers-in-training have no autobiographical experiences so outstanding that their life story is of interest to others. Likewise, they do not have any experience so extraordinary or so dangerous or so romantic or so unusual as to warrant a partial autobiography. (A professional writer and author of books on writing)

This attitude is challenged by a wave of new women writers as well as some older established women writers. Henry James, one of a handful of male writers who were allies, said:

> The women novelists had done better than the men in reminding them of man's relations with himself, that is, with women.... His relations with the pistol, the police, the wild and the tame beast—are not these prevailingly what the gentlemen have given us?

Everyday life, problems of all kinds, people of all kinds, are all story material, all important.

Willa Cather said of Katherine Mansfield:

> It was usually Miss Mansfield's way to approach the major forces of life through comparatively trivial incidents. She chose a small reflector to throw a luminous streak out into the shadowy realm of personal relationships, the seemingly unimportant ones interested her the most.

So don't be misled into believing your idea is not important. If it's important to you, and you can communicate it to others, you have a book.

PLANNING YOUR STORY

There are writers who don't plan or polish. That's a way of writing, and if you prefer it, and it works for you, you can skip this section.

Most writers do some organizing. As you develop your skill, you'll probably do it less, unless you are the methodical type, or the material demands it.

Decide first on the type, style, and form. Then develop a synopsis or skeleton outline, as you would tell it to a stranger who asks, "What is your book about?"

Next, break it down into chapters. Depending on the material, there may be parts I and II, or even more. If it's an article, do an outline of the paragraphs to see the progression of the idea.

LENGTH AND SELECTION

All writing is selection. Sometimes it's hard to leave out a favorite event. But too much material can be confusing and block the flow of the story. Sometimes you'll have to weigh simplicity against richness. What is clutter in one place in the writing may be enhancement in another. Details or daily habits, methods of work, fantasies, reflections, are often links that strengthen your bond with the reader.

A nonfiction book, double-spaced and typewritten, can be anything from eighty to eight hundred pages. The length of articles is undefined—from one page and up, depending on the type and the target magazine.

STRUCTURE

Your outline is the blueprint of how the story is proportioned. Unity and consistency need to be thought of in terms of where to place certain episodes and ideas. But don't be too rigid. You have outlined a story goal, but if you feel the urge to veer off in another direction, go with it and see where it takes you. You can adjust the story to it later.

In the final plan, unity of many elements needs to be established. There is unity of statement. Keep asking, "What point do I want to make here?" "Am I sticking to the original purpose of the book?"

For unity of style, decide whether it is to be impersonal, casual, formal, humorous, intense, light, or philosophical. One will dominate, others are for relief and variety.

Lastly, watch your tenses. "Is," "was," "has," or "had been," have a way of getting mixed up.

THE TITLE, BEGINNING, MIDDLE, AND ENDING

Briefly, the opening tells the reader what to expect, the middle fulfills the promise, and the ending pulls everything together and emphasizes the statement. The two problems that puzzle most autobiographers are how to begin the story and how to end it.

The opening is the most important part of your book. It must capture the reader's interest. The first thing the reader will see is the title. It's the way the book is identified, and it shouldn't deceive the reader. The story should do what the title says. If it is a fragment of a provocative idea, readers will look for completion. For example, "Center Stage" suggests an author or an actress, but who? Where? What about it?

A major problem for autobiographers in terms of the opening is what time of life to begin the story. Chronological works begin at birth. Family histories begin as far back as ancestry can be traced. But stories can begin any time from when you were a gleam in your mother's eye to the night of your conception (Sacha Guitry used this to show *why* he was born), in adolescence, or at the moment you sit down to write, using flashbacks in historical sequence or at random. This is where your own imagination can take flight.

A strong way to begin is at the pivotal point of your selected story, such as marriage, the launching of a career, or any high point when your feelings were most intense, and what meant the most to you. Then use flashbacks to past events, returning intermittently to the present to comment. This creates a richness in self-portraiture.

Axel Munthe, the Swedish doctor who wrote his autobiography in the early 1920s, called it *The Story of San Michele,* the villa he built in Anacapri on the site of the ruins of the palace of Emperor Tiberius. It was his later life's preoccupation. He appropriately begins his story on arrival at his *place:*

> I sprang from the Sorrento sailing-boat on to the little beach. Swarms of boys were playing about among the upturned boats or bathing their shining bronze bodies in the surf, and old fishermen in red Phrygian caps sat mending their nets outside their boathouses.

Jean-Pierre Aumont, the French actor, in his autobiography, *Sun and Shadow,* doesn't make us guess what his passion and his book are about:

> I was born at the age of sixteen. Is there any other birth for an actor than the first day he finds himself standing in the wings of a theater?

At whichever point in your life you decide to begin, it is the shuttling back and forth from past to present that most fascinates scholars and psychologists—how the present person relates to the many selves along the way in his development. Ask yourself, will you write what was important *as* a child, from the child's point of view? Or will it be to demonstrate how past events made you what you are today? Or as if you were reliving it? Ask yourself many questions and pin yourself down to answers, and the manner of opening your story will evolve.

The opening sentence and paragraph, or the lead, are the most important in the entire book. It's the lure to read on. It's a hook and a promise. It's your story in microcosm. You have a wide choice of types—an anecdote, lines of dialogue, a description, a quotation, a dynamic narrative, or any other kind of striking sentence, even one for pure shock value. But don't take too long to get to the point. In a book, you can take a little longer to get started than with an article, but no more than a page or two.

The middle explains and expands the opening. The bulk of it is a series of events like scenes in fiction. These are held together by narration, and exposition. Dialogue and description add color, interest, and variety.

Watch your *transitions* from one scene to another, one point to another. Don't be afraid to use the simple basic connectives such as "but," "anyway," "besides," and "finally." It's a question of keeping a smooth flow and not disorienting the reader by jumping too abruptly from one thing to another. Continue to use hooks such as questions, novelty, humor, surprises, intriguing points, strong statements, and the use of everyday, familiar experiences to make the readers feel that you have taken them into your confidence.

Most important is that your story builds and doesn't let the reader down at the end. Take pains with the continuity, and don't use up all your best stuff too soon.

Keep your synopsis handy as a guide. Make notes on it as you think of new ideas.

The ending is what will remain with the readers. *How* do you want to leave them? Laughing, crying, thinking, contemplating, angry? Decide this in advance. If the ending paragraph and sentence don't come to you now, they will along the way. Jot down ideas as they occur to you. Lines have a way of evaporating from memory.

Favorite types of endings are anecdotes, dialogue, and apt quotations. In some, there is the feeling that this is merely a "slice of life" and that the author's life will continue as before.

Pearl Buck, in ending *My Several Worlds*, only pauses:

> In this mood of faith and hope my work goes on. A ream of fresh paper lies on my desk waiting for the next book. I am a writer and I take up my pen to write—

Gertrude Stein's autobiography, written as *The Autobiography of Alice B. Toklas* (as though written by Toklas, her companion of twenty-five years), ends with the straightforwardness of her history-making style:

> About six weeks ago Gertrude Stein said, it does not look to me as if you were ever going to write that autobiography. You know what I am going to do. I am going to write it for you. I am going to write it as simply as Defoe did the autobiography of Robinson Crusoe. And she has and this is it.

A surprise ending is extremely effective because it stirs up an extra measure of emotion to offset the feeling of loss when a book comes to an end. Sometimes it's used to pick up a "down" ending. One by Merle Miller and Evan Rhodes illustrates this, in *Only You, Dick Daring!* The book is a "true-life adventure" about working on a TV pilot film, written in a light comedy style. The undercurrent is a horror story of the machinations of the TV industry and how Miller's and Rhodes's project was dropped abruptly after it was filmed. They end with an unexpected telephone call from their agent:

> "Hello, Harold," I heard Evan say. "No, he's not. He's out walking in the woods . . ."
> I picked up the phone in the study. "Hi, Harold."
> "Merle, I know how you feel about a television series, but when I heard about this one, I said, 'There's only one writer in America' . . . and this is going to be a multimillion dollar . . . World War II is very big right now . . . you write so well about the war, and . . ."
> "No, Harold."

In the ending, emphasize your statement in a subtle, personal way. Don't sum up obviously such as "What I guess I was trying to say in this book is . . ." Let the readers sum up for themselves. If they don't know what it was about by now, it's too late.

If you plan a sequel, don't leave the readers with questions about it. They are left hanging, uncomfortable, unsatisfied. Your next book may not be available for years!

Most important, don't drag it out. Make your point, but don't hammer it in. Know when to stop.

EXERCISE 1. WHERE TO BEGIN _____

PURPOSE OF THIS EXERCISE
To practice writing opening and closing lines, and to explore alternatives for types of autobiographies possible with your material.

INSTRUCTIONS
1. Imagine you have decided to do a panoramic autobiography. Write a *paragraph* for each of the following:
   a. Your opening
   b. A major turning point in the story
   c. The ending

2. The same as above, but this time imagine you have decided to do a thematic autobiography. In choosing, ask yourself, "What is the most important topic in my life? Work? A special accomplishment? An experience? Obstacles overcome? Romance?"

3. Write *one sentence* each for *three* "seed plots" which suggest themselves from the above exercise so far.

EXAMPLE (A STUDENT, AN OLDER WOMAN):
   1. Panoramic autobiography
      a. (Opening) If I had listened to what most people told me, I never would have accomplished anything.

      b. (A major turning point) Everyone was told to turn back, that to drive in such a blizzard was asking for trouble. But something told me to risk it. I had to go on.

      c. (The ending) I often think that it would have been better to behave like an average person, and not take such big risks. But there's no way I can do the things I do so well without having gone through all that. I wouldn't change a minute of my life.

2. A thematic autobiography

      a. (Opening) Finding one's true path is easy for some, but for me, becoming a college teacher has been the most surprising and nerve-wracking accomplishment of my life.

      b. (Turning point) I had to ask myself whether it was worth going on, or throwing away seven years of hard work.

      c. (The ending) All doubts have been demolished about my true path in life. Teaching is second nature to me now.

EXERCISE 2. LETTER TO THE EDITOR⎯⎯⎯⎯⎯⎯

PURPOSE OF THIS EXERCISE

This will begin to build your confidence in stating your opinions. It will also help you clarify your thinking on a subject you feel strongly about, especially if you are emotional about it.

This will also help you build your courage to submit material for publication.

INSTRUCTIONS

Read the "Letters to the Editor" column in your local newspaper every day, for six days. Jot down ideas about your feelings and opinions on topics in the news, or any related ideas as they come to mind.

On the seventh day, choose a subject. In ten lines or less,

write a letter to the editor, expressing a strong opinion about a current social condition you feel should be improved or changed, something that would improve your life or the lives of a special group of people, or anything else.

For the first letter, choose the topic that evokes the strongest emotion in you. Write one of these letters every week.

EXAMPLE (AN OLDER COLLEGE STUDENT):

> *Dear Editor:*
>
> *Isn't it time the public stopped being interested in items such as "Prince Charles buys a new horse?"*
>
> *Samuel Adams, the Father of the American Revolution, said that if we don't get rid of the royalists, we'll be in trouble. And we are.*
>
> *Royalty assaults us wherever we turn.*
>
> *Isn't it time we remembered that we fought a revolution to rid ourselves of royal oppression?*
>
> *Yours truly,*

READINGS

BOMBECK, ERMA. *If Life Is a Bowl of Cherries, What Am I Doing in the Pits?* New York: Fawcett Crest, 1978. Space won't permit a list of the works of this most popular humorist. She deals with everyday events and issues from the housewife's point of view, injecting dynamic statements.

BUCK, PEARL. *My Several Worlds.* New York: The John Day Co., 1954. An exciting life and a beautifully told story by one of America's finest writers.

CAINE, LYNN. *Widow.* New York: William Sloane Associates, 1964. A widow's story of what it's like to raise children alone and to deal with the emotional problems of this situation.

DEAN, JOHN W., III. *Blind Ambition: The White House Years.* New York: Simon & Schuster, 1976. Dean's struggle with his conscience is the basis for this thematic and partial autobiography.

FRANKLIN, BENJAMIN. *The Autobiography of Benjamin Franklin.* New York: A. S. Barnes & Co., 1944. A wonderful classic. Basic reading for the autobiographer who wants to be well organized.

GANDHI, MOHANDAS K. *An Autobiography.* Boston: Beacon Press, 1957. "Must" reading for those who wish to do a panoramic and thematic book.

HERRIGEL, EUGEN. *Zen in the Art of Archery.* New York: Pantheon Books, 1953. An experience in a Buddhist monastery. Excellent.

MANSFIELD, KATHERINE. *The Journal of Katherine Mansfield.* New York: Alfred A. Knopf, 1927. Mansfield defied convention and became famous as a short-story writer as well.

MCCARTHY, MARY. *Memories of a Catholic Girlhood.* New York: Harcourt, Brace & World, 1952. Experience in spiritual growth and life in a convent school.

MUNTHE, AXEL. *The Story of San Michele.* London: The Albatross, 1948. An exceptional book about a Swedish doctor's dream of building a house on the site of the Emperor Tiberius' palace.

11

Fiction

Every human being is a plot.

—LEO TOLSTOY

Beneath the American Dream of mansions, fast cars, designer clothes, sexual attraction, and public acclaim, is another dream: to write the great American novel.

This dream is visualized in a modest-to-poverty monk-like setting, a version of the artist's garret in which material pleasures are renounced for the spiritual values of art, quality of life, true friendship, and love.

Dream number 1, of fame and fortune, is a media-manufactured product, and dream number 2 suggests the real American crying to be let out. Writing seems a safe way to begin the process of emancipation.

Almost everyone, at some time or another, expresses a desire to write, and fiction is thought to be synonymous with "true" writing.

An even more secret longing is dream number 2A: to write a play—secret because while the novel has somewhat overcome the bias of "mystique" as more and more "ordinary" people succeed in producing very good novels, the dramatic play form is still overprotected by a professional clique. In no other field do the tentacles of bias grip more unyieldingly than in playwriting. The dramatist is "born, not made," to write a successful play requires a special talent "which is not capable of being imparted," "and either you have it in you or you don't," are a few warnings from leading authorities.

In spite of their harshness to invaders of the general fiction field, books about writing offer valuable guidance, if you haven't been turned back by page 2. The way to deal with this is to *assume you have a measure of talent that can be developed.*

There are dynamic reasons for considering fiction to tell your story. It has some attractive advantages and a broad spectrum of form. Sometimes the only way you can tell your story is to disguise it as fiction. Marcel Proust said, "You can tell anything, but on condition that you never say 'I'!"

There may be people in your life you'd like to portray as mildly objectionable to obnoxious, but you're afraid they'll recognize themselves. Don't worry—people don't usually identify with such characters.

The fictional form is also desirable as you dredge through material you have been avoiding, material too painful to handle frontally. The third-person or objective point of view is an oblique way to review those difficult times. When you look at the past through the eyes of a storyteller, you can see patterns and meanings in events that you couldn't at the moment of your emotional involvement.

Through fiction you can examine your latent potentials. In creating situations for your counterpart in a story, you can illuminate your future by imagining, for example, "If I had had these opportunities, I could have . . ."

Fiction offers unlimited opportunity to fulfill (in writing) fantasies of sex, beauty, brilliance, luxury, fame. Aggression worked out on paper often remains there. The same is true of revenge. You can carry this to the extreme and kill someone— in your story—destroy him in your psyche so he will haunt you no more. You can discover the mechanics of the situation that produced such intense feeling, and you can examine the situation from both sides—yours and his.

Fiction allows you to say anything you please, without fear of ridicule or reprisal. You can be your total self, accepting your light side, dark side, and the shades in between; in fiction they can be more fully explored than you usually do in real life.

Through fiction you can expand still further. You can explore different roles, take on different identities, try combinations of personalities yet undeveloped. For example, you might ask, "What if I, with my talent for cooking, had my sister Irene's business ability, and my friend Peter's personality—I could run a successful restaurant." (A long-standing dream, but one you have considered hopeless.) Carry this idea into the story, research the components necessary to accomplish this goal, and how the characters ran into the common hazards of the trade. Put yourself in Irene's place, through a character. As she works out the business details, you may find that business acumen is not as formidable as you thought. Putting yourself inside Peter's personality can bring out yours as you see how an outgoing personality like his operates in action.

In the nonfiction autobiography you must stick to being yourself and to seeing your life from the inside. Fiction has no such limitations. You can get *outside* yourself and inside others. You can decide what others are thinking and feeling, not just guess at it. The central character (yourself, or a version of yourself) can be described by others in the story. In the nonfiction autobiography there are always some things hidden, as there are in life. In fiction, memories, hidden or open, are no longer a problem. Scenes are as fresh as the moment they were lived, not dimmed or distorted through the screens of memory.

The central character's life can be completed. The character can follow through on any action that you, in life, were not able to. Nothing is cut short, thwarted, unfulfilled, as it is in life, unless the story dictates these obstacles for the sake of suspense. There is a sense of freedom in being able to manipulate the facts of your life. A story can be created from a fragment of an impression or expanded to a majestic chronicle spanning many centuries. It is still your story. The major common denominator between fiction and nonfiction is the *meaning* of the story you tell.

Anyone can learn the fundamentals of fiction. Even the strictest instructor of the "born writer" persuasion will admit to certain elements inherent in good writing and will agree that they can be learned. The beginning writer can, at least, save years of trial and error.

Craft is a product of the conscious mind. The *art* of writing arises from the unconscious. As far as we know, this is the part that cannot be taught because it is the distinctive personal mark the individual brings to a project. Dorothea Brande, in *Becoming a Writer*, says of this:

> The unconscious must flow freely, richly, bringing at demand all the treasures of memory, all the emotions, incidents, scenes, intimations of character and relationship which it has stored away in its depths; the conscious mind must control, combine and discriminate between these materials and without hampering the unconscious flow.

The writer's conscious mind serves as critic, teacher, nurturer, and cheerleader to himself. It sorts and structures material. After a while, the conscious and unconscious will work cooperatively in that seamless unity of the trained artist. There is a time to let ideas flow, a "creative trauma" to run its course, unchecked. It actually feels like a state of trance, after which one "awakens" to a piece of work, half aware of having done it. Then there is a time to put the conscious mind to work and arrange this material in its best showcase.

One school of writing doesn't believe in anything *but* the product of the creative trauma process, claiming that this product alone is art, and that it shouldn't be tampered with. Another school doesn't believe in anything but the conscious effort of putting a story together by principles of craft. This is known as the "recipe-book" method of writing, resulting in a "cookie-cutter" product. It is comparable to learning to draw by connecting dots or painting by numbers. The products of these extreme approaches are not found among the most lasting literature.

Fiction is so vast and complex that the terminology alone would fill a book with its categories and confusions. I shall only attempt to select concepts basic to all fiction and useful mainly for writing autobiographical fiction. Then I'll offer a few pointers about three major forms: the novel, the short story, and the dramatic forms. I've chosen the terms and concepts that writers were most comfortable with in workshops.

First, what is fiction? A folklore definition is that fiction is telling lies, but with truths. The definition (or more accurately, the description) agreed on by most professionals is that fiction is telling a story, and a story is *an action designed in time*.

The action is a struggle between two opposing forces: the

protagonist (hero or heroine) versus the antagonist (the villain). It can be between two people, or a person against the elements, a mysterious unseen force, social conditions, or illness, or an inner struggle within the protagonist.

The storyteller's skill is to feed the reader's response to a primitive urge to know, "What next? Then what? And then ...and then...?" E. M. Forster calls it "the literary tapeworm." This curiosity is what stories must stimulate, and this is what form is all about—to help achieve it. Whether the action takes place in a time span of thirty minutes or three hundred years, the reader's curiosity is grabbed at once. Maugham says:

> Form for the poet is the bit and bridle without which (unless you are an acrobat) you cannot ride your horse; but for the writer of prose it is the chassis without which your car does not exist.

It's best to begin with established forms. Develop a solid base of technique and adeptness with the tools of the trade before taking off into uncharted terrain. Historically, fiction writers have had their best success becoming well grounded in the knowns before they developed their sometimes radically individual styles. Kenneth Macgowan said that the apprentice playwright:

> must learn to walk the road of conventional dramaturgy before he can safely run the byways of theatrical experimentation. Picasso was a master of draftsmanship before he began to experiment with cubism.

John Van Druten, a leading playwright, concurred:

> I am inclined to think that an acquaintance with the older rules of the well-made play is still a good basis for learning how to break them.

I'll use four major headings to block out the principles of craft—just to keep theory simple. They'll be as follows: Characters, The Story, The Plot, and Structure and Style.

CHARACTERS

I begin with characters because students who designed their stories around characters found this the easiest way to begin, and for the autobiographer it's the most natural. It's one of the points on which authorities agree:

> *Characters Make Your Story.* (Book by Maren Elwood, writing teacher)

> Plot can never make characters; the writer must find or create the people that animate a story. But characters can and do make a plot. (Kenneth Macgowan)

> I have taken living people and put them into the situations, tragic or comic, that their characters suggested. I might well say that they invented their own stories. (Somerset Maugham)

As autobiographer, you are ahead of the game. You already know your characters well, only too well, you may say. The task, then, is how to select, adapt, emphasize, and combine. The final characters will be composites. As you develop your story and a character seems to get lost or become less relevant to the plot, cut him out or fuse him with another.

One way to begin a story is to sit down with the characters you plan to use and describe each one in detail.

PROTAGONIST OR CENTRAL CHARACTER

You can emphasize a quality you understand well about yourself and minimize something about yourself you don't fathom.

The *antagonist* should be an equal or stronger force at first. He's there to test the protagonist. He may be an O.K. person, but he's not O.K. in the story. He's there to add color. His character doesn't usually vacillate—he doesn't let up on his single-minded goal.

Unity of personality is the closest thing to a hard rule there is. The reader must believe that *this* person would do *this* thing. Every action should support this selfness. Though a person is multifaceted, in life and fiction, he is of interest to the story through the emphasis of a dominant trait, a dominant emotion. Think carefully, too, about the emotional effect you want a character to have on the reader, and see that it is consistent in his action, or if it changes, that it changes with a story purpose and with clarity. Even the name you choose should match the personality and tell the reader something about him immediately.

Introduce characters in order of their importance to the story. This orients the reader. If you don't do this, there ought to be a good reason why, for the story's sake.

Develop your characters as the story moves along. You don't want the reader to know them all at once. As the plot unfolds, the characters are confronted with situations designed to disclose more and more of themselves and their modes of interacting with one another.

DESCRIPTION AND DETAIL

There are three types. *Concrete* description shows the reader what you see, objectively. "She moved slowly, turning her head to each side with each coordinated arm and leg swing." The reader makes up his own mind about what he visualizes. *Figurative* description uses similes and metaphors. "She moved like a young reindeer, alert to possible danger." This tells something about the character; a self-defensive characteristic. *Abstract* description gives the author's judgment of a character. "Her cautious movements, one slow step at a time, a look to the right, then to the left, gave a paranoid cast to her interaction and made me feel distrusted." Though abstract description is considered author intrusion, it's often a necessary device to push a story along. Most stories are a blend of all three.

For variety, one character may describe another. This may give information about both.

Use detail. The drop of an eyelid, the way he lights a cigarette, drives a car, can tell us more about a character than a paragraph of dry description.

Do a *character profile,* writing down everything you can think of to round out the character. You won't use all the material in the story, but you'll know it, and you'll have the person act and react with a feeling of totality and depth. You can even paste a photograph on this page, or draw a sketch of a character you are inventing. If you are combining two characters, use a photo and a projected likeness of the final character, as though you were illustrating the story.

First, write down vital statistics: name, birth date, age, sex, height and weight, color of eyes, skin, and hair, type of posture, manner of dress, special gestures, voice, details such as birthmarks or scars. Describe social status, whether lower, middle, or upper class, and background. Also type of occupation, hobbies, political bent, prejudices. Education—which schools, favorite subjects, kinds of grades, aptitudes. What kind of home life— what kind of parents, siblings, relationships with family. Religion. Active in community. Kinds of books he reads, movies he goes to. Entertains, joins clubs. Types of friends. Psychological traits are most important in terms of underlying motivations. Tell about sex life, moral standards, what he wants out of life, frustrations, goals, satisfactions, disappointments. What kind of temperament, whether placid, trigger temper, pessimistic or optimistic, bitter, loving, giving, a taker or giver. Any complexes, phobias. Extrovert or introvert. Talents, major or minor. Intellectual capacity, imagination, creativity, sense of judgment, sense of humor.

Do all this for your own information, saturating yourself in your book-people. When you begin to actually write it, however, don't prolong descriptions or statements unless necessary, or very interesting. Descriptions can hard-pack information into a few lines.

Study the work of writers you admire. Dissect each sentence to see how it gives subtle or direct information about their characters while showing us how they look.

MOTIVATION

In a story, this is individualized for the special characters. Basic drives are those such as hunger, self-preservation, safety, self-defense, sex. Higher needs are love, loyalty, gratitude, altruism, right thinking and action, to do good work. The central character will have an objective that the antagonist will try to prevent him from achieving, or interfere with directly (unaware that he is doing it), or the antagonist will have the same goal in competition with the protagonist.

Major and minor characters sometimes shift their positions in a story as the plot is developed. Some authors, like

E. M. Forster, feel that characters should be "round" or "flat."
Round refers to a fully developed personality, seen from all
sides. *Flat* characters have a single trait. Forster said:

> One great advantage of flat characters is that they are
> easily recognized when ever they come in . . . they are
> easily remembered by the reader afterwards . . . they were
> not changed by circumstance. . . . A novel that is at all
> complex often requires flat people as well as round.

Norman Douglas, a foremost writer, disagrees, stating that
the use of flat characters "consists, I should say, in a failure to
realize the complexities of the ordinary human mind."

Choose whichever theory suits your story and inclination
toward the various characters. Simplified theory holds that vil-
lains are usually flat. Short stories are limited in time to develop
round people, but as you develop writing skill, characters can be
rounded by concise description, bits of dialogue, and other elements of craft.

DIALOGUE

This is the beginning writer's bugaboo. They either attempt
Shakespearean tones, or reproduce "natural" dialogue that
sounds stiff. For the playwright, of course, dialogue must be
mastered. In any form of writing, it is a major link to the understanding of characters. We get to know them by their
choice of words, accents, the way they handle language, and
tone of voice. The best way to practice writing dialogue is to
listen, become an eavesdropper, and write down individual
styles of speech on buses, in restaurants, wherever you go.
Write them down exactly as you heard them. Later, review and
adapt to a story character. Record and transcribe anyone who
has an interesting accent or type of speech. Start a collection
of tapes. Record *yourself* speaking as you would imagine a
character saying a line. Here are some points to mull over
when you write dialogue:

> If long speeches are necessary, inject an occasional com-
> ment from another person so we know they're still
> there.

Don't get carried away with brilliant wordage if it takes attention away from the story line.

The main functions are to advance the plot, reveal character, give necessary information, and be interesting of itself.

POINT OF VIEW

This is the question of who is speaking as the author. The first-person point of view, using *I,* as though it were an autobiography, has the advantage of a you-are-there effect. It has some limitations of the nonfiction autobiography, but we can't rigidly rule out the idea. It has been successfully executed, from Charlotte Brontë's *Jane Eyre* to Erica Jong's *Fear of Flying.*

The third-person point of view is the most popular and the most dramatic. It is the most appropriate for the autobiographer using fiction form. The reader gets a ringside view of the entire action, as the author becomes a "camera eye." An extended version of this is the *"omniscient"* point of view that lets you go inside the head of any or all the characters and see the action from any character's point of view. Some authorities feel that once a point of view is established, it should be consistent. Percy Lubbock, in *The Craft of Fiction,* deplores the book that shifts points of view and believes that Tolstoy's *War and Peace* missed its true greatness because of it. E. M. Forster disagrees: "A novelist can shift his point of view if it comes off, and it came off with Dickens and Tolstoy."

CHARACTERS IN THEIR SETTINGS

I'm including this along with characters because setting is important as background to the character. By selection of a setting, a mood can be established immediately as positive or negative. A storm suggests trouble, a beautiful day happiness. But consistency with the story applies. There might have been thunder and lightning on the day you were married in real life. But if the story calls for a peaceful wedding, this setting would confuse the mood.

The classic way of introducing a setting is to first describe the part of it that sets off the character and then move outward so that your character isn't chopped off abruptly, but kept attached to the environment. The most important thing about setting is to let your reader know where the action is taking place at all times. The simplest way to do this is to introduce it at the beginning of each scene. "Back at the ranch . . ." may be corny, but it's clear.

THE STORY

Theories about story ideas range from the simplistic Hollywood love-story formula of "Boy meets girl, boy loses girl, boy gets girl"—or, as in theater, "In Act I get him up a tree, in Act II throw rocks at him, and in Act III get him down"—to the most complex definitions and rules for plotting, complete with diagrams in the shape of half-circles, pyramids, and arrowheads. Even simpler is the belief that you can do anything providing it is interesting by the "What happens next?" system.

Terms and definitions vary from book to book, so I have chosen those which seemed most helpful and simple in building a story by progressive steps.

TYPES OF STORIES

By E. M. Forster's definition, "A story is a narrative of events arranged in their time and sequence." The protagonist wants something and either gets it or doesn't. There are two types:

1. Accomplishes mission.
    a. Through ingenuity. Show that he was born with it. Establish it early. He figures it out instead of fighting it out.
    b. By a special capacity. Give its background, how it was acquired. Inject some technical facts for authenticity.
    c. With a weapon, actual or figurative. It can be anything, but one that he would use and something tangible. The more ingenious, the more powerful the action.
    d. With courage, physical or moral.

2. Does not accomplish mission.
    a. Accepts defeat and compensates for it. Don't show him as weak or inviting pity. And he must *never* pity himself.

  b. He abandons objective because it wasn't real or
     right. Develop him as the type of person who
     would change his mind.

STORY IDEA, GERM, OR CORE

This tells the kind of action it is. The verb is the key: "A woman *searches* for her natural parents." Most books about writing agree that story ideas should be taken from life. If you're still concerned about your life being ordinary, become aware that most fiction is about ordinary people. Maugham said:

> The ordinary is the writer's richer field. Its unexpected-
> ness, its singularity, its infinite variety afford unending
> material. The great man is too often all of a piece; it is the
> little man that is a bundle of contradictory elements. He is
> inexhaustible. You never come to the end of the surprises
> he has in store for you. For my part I would much sooner
> spend a month on a desert island with a veterinary surgeon
> than with a prime minister.

"Face the fear of hidden embarrassments forthrightly and take the subjects for your first stories from your own life," said R. V. Cassill, teacher and author.

The foundation of autobiographical fiction is to *write what you know,* and about where, what, and whom you know. Examples are abundant. Elia Kazan's novel *Acts of Love* "does acknowledge an autobiographical interest." "I like this woman," he said of his character, Ethel, "There's more of me in her than appears." Lili Palmer, after the success of her autobiography, *Change Lobsters and Dance,* wrote a novel, *Red Raven,* which she called autobiographical fiction and in which she told what she could not in the first book. Among the classics, Charlotte Brontë's *Jane Eyre* parallels the major events of her life, and later the novel *Villette* plays out and fulfills a love she could not in her private life. D. H. Lawrence wrote *Sons and Lovers* to come to terms with his past as it was expressed in a love relationship. James Joyce's *Portrait of the Artist as a Young Man* fulfills the promise of the title. He sees himself only as an artist: he sees the world revolving around himself, admittedly undeveloped in feelings, and believes that the creation of art is all that matters.

THE THEME

This is the moral to the story. For example, for the seed plot "A woman searches for her natural parents," her search may lead to problems of racial origin and evolve a theme such as: "In spite of political advances, racial prejudice remains a major social problem."

THE PLOT

Think of plotting as planning. Once your story idea is formulated, your plot can begin to take shape. The plot, said Forster, is also a narrative of events like the story, but "the emphasis falls on causality." Where a story answers, "Then what?" the plot answers, "Why?" The protagonist realizes or resolves something, but does so visibly and dramatically. The principles discussed in Chapter 10 on nonfiction hold true for fiction, with a few variations. In fiction, the structure is more contained in design and the action intensified. The closer the protagonist comes to losing, the greater the drama. In nonfiction, the general emotion is "Ah, yes, such is life." Fiction is an impression of life and touches a heightened state of consciousness. A simple diagram of formal plotting contains the following:

1. Problem		Beginning (Exposition)
2. Complication		
3. Crisis		
4. Decision	Climax	Body (Development)
5. Sacrifice		
6. Final Conflict		
7. Solution		End (Resolution)
8. Reward		

THE BEGINNING

This constitutes approximately one-fourth of the story. Open at the most interesting time. Introduce all main characters in order of importance. Establish the type of story, what it's about, and key information about characters and their relationships. Establish the physical setting. Put the protagonist in action as soon as possible. He should be as strong as the antagonist. The antagonist should declare his intentions up front. Don't labor over making this too subtle. The reader should know the main problem right away.

THE MIDDLE

This is the body or development of the story. All story characters and situations have been introduced. Don't bring in an important point or person late. As the protagonist moves toward the goal, he is stopped. He is in a worse situation than before. Complications, obstacles, and small crises begin to pile up. A decision must be made. The protagonist must act against seemingly impossible odds. He must risk or sacrifice something, or be ready to do so. He makes the big move, but is faced with the biggest obstacle. It appears that the antagonist is going to win. This is when the protagonist is a "cliff hanger," and his rope is beginning to break literally or figuratively. It doesn't seem possible for him to escape.

THE ENDING

This part begins immediately after the big crisis or climax. The protagonist proves himself to be a hero. The obligatory scene is the one in which he does what he said he would do. In the *denouement,* the problem is solved. All loose ends are tied up. There is usually a reward.

STRUCTURE AND STYLE

In the autobiography, there will be some descriptions of events in which you did not actively participate. In fiction, there is "off-stage" action, described in the narrative sections. This brings the reader up to date. Most of the action, though, is visible. The motto of fiction is "Show them, don't tell them." Give necessary information to introduce the story and fill in the cracks as you go along. It isn't important to get fancy or subtle or ingenious in doing this. It's more important to state this information clearly. I've chosen five general areas to be aware of: unity, style, scenes, narration, and transitions.

UNITY

Unity and economy of language go hand in hand. If a part of the story is overwritten, unity is disturbed. Watch for unity in the following areas:

1. *Time.* The reader should know how much time has passed at each story point. The time span should be kept at the minimum necessary for clarity and story purpose. Time is a device for suspense, so don't lose your reader for a moment, or the spell will be broken.

2. *Place.* Unless you have plenty of time in which to tell your story, such as a panoramic novel, it's better not to bounce around in many locations. Don't make a radical change in location unless it's integrated into the story.

3. *Action.* This is most important. It should be continuous, contained, complete, and single—one action at a time.

4. *Character.* As was discussed earlier, each person in the story should be faithful to his character.

5. *Overall story effect.* The story is most powerful if it has a dominant effect, and achieves it cumulatively.

STYLE

This is what you bring to a story that no one else can do as well. No one can do it for you. Certain elements compose style, but it is the *way* you put them together that produces the final effect.

1. *Pattern.* What shape or symbol your story suggests—a tree, a heavy chain, a bubble bath. What painter or composer you would choose as background.

2. *Rhythm.* Whether the story hurries along or has a lingering ebb and flow. The luxury of a symphony or a clear, condensed statement like a sonata. It can be a hummable-tune type of story.

3. *Tempo.* The speed of your prose. *Pace* is the speed of the action. You can slow the reader down to reflect—by choice of words, word sequence, punctuation.

4. *Mood.* Created by specific detail, color, the elements (rain, fire), nostalgia, mode of description, interplay between narration and scenes. The reader is putty in the hands of a writer who can create mood and evoke emotion.

Don't overload a story with style. Weave it into the texture, and don't allow it to fuzz up the clarity of your thoughts.

SCENES

The scene is the dramatic unit of presentation. The height of dramatic writing is to create the feeling that the reader is there, is a minor character, observing. In memory, we recall scenes of the past. In fantasy, we image scenes of the future. It accomplishes what a camera or stage scene does. A complete scene pushes the action forward as a plot step. The time span is uninterrupted. There is some kind of confrontation. The complete scene is used only for high points of the story. Another type of scene is the half-scene. This needn't be a complete action, but it uses touches of dialogue for variety, description, or mood.

Basic scene purposes are:

1. To get an object (inanimate, nonhuman).

2. To give or dispose of an object.

3. To get specific information.

4. To give specific information.

5. To get a consent or reply.

6. To give a consent or reply.

7. To preserve some object, creature, or person.

8. To destroy some object, creature, or person.

9. To discover or uncover some circumstance or set of them.

10. To reveal some circumstance or set of them.

11. To create, establish, confirm, or force some action, behavior, or attitude.

12. To deny an action, behavior, or attitude.

Any of these basic scenes can end in one of these ways: (a) achievement (b) failure (c) abandonment.

NARRATION

Narrative passages are subject to differing points of view by writers and teachers. One formal view is that they tell what characters do, but many other uses are described: to condense time spans, to insert tantalizing clues, to review the story periodically or summarize, to change the pace, to prepare for scenes and serve as contrast to the close-up and detailed view of scenes, to dispense duller information sandwiched in between more interesting information, to explain characters and situations, and at all times to keep the reader oriented.

TRANSITIONS

Keep a smooth flow to the story from one passage to the next. There are transitions of time, place, mood, tempo, and viewpoint. The classic way of writing a transition is indirectly, by having a character perform a small act or gesture relating to the scene or narrative. For example, if a meadow is described, a character can lean down to pick a flower in it. Then pick up another character somewhere else and go on with the story. With this device, the scene has a subtle closure, and does not chop off a person. It is also correct to pick up with a "back at the ranch" phrase to put the next passage in immediate action. In the short story, the use of a simple word or phrase is important when there is not enough time to stretch out scenes with the leisure that a novel permits.

THE NOVEL

There is no way to define a novel. Henry James would not accept any restrictions of form on the novelist's art. He said:

> (Critics) would argue, of course, that a novel ought to be good, but they would interpret this term in a fashion of their own, which indeed would vary considerably from one critic to another.

The majority of successful novelists and most teachers would agree. The truth is, there *are* writers who sit down and write without attention to form or even much planning, and there are others who plan precisely along established lines. Neither approach to the novel is right or wrong. They both produce "good" and "bad" novels. Find the system that works best for your temperament and style. This discussion of craft has been mostly about "formula" writing—forms and molds and principles that have been tried and true to gain special effects. You will have to work at it. Don't go by theory alone. Experiment with methods—in action.

R. V. Cassill said:

> If you don't begin until you have all available theory in your mind, you may never get a story on paper. Moreover, it is three times as easy to absorb theory if you are making efforts of your own to which it can be related.

Mainly, you can put more of yourself in the novel than in any other form. It is not totally dependent on the crisis. The in-betweens of the action are as important. The bulk of the novel is an elaboration of your theme. In the novel, you can role-play to the hilt, and through any character or composite, you can struggle to the end of your endurance, whirl off the complete range of your emotional repertory, and then follow through any action to the highest peak your imagination will take you. In short, it offers unlimited opportunity to probe human consciousness and behavior. E. M. Forster said:

> No English novelist is as great as Tolstoy—that is to say has given so complete a picture of man's life, both on its

domestic and heroic side. No English novelist has explored man's soul as deeply as Dostoevsky. And no novelist anywhere has analyzed the modern consciousness as Marcel Proust.

Forster agrees with Henry James who said: "The only obligation to which in advance we may hold the novel is that it be interesting." He gives us a clue to the mechanics of how this is accomplished:

> The specialty of the novel is that the writer can talk about his characters as well as through them or can arrange for us to listen when they talk to themselves. He has access to self-communions, and from that level he can descend even deeper and peer into the subconscious.

Are we to believe, then, that a novel that doesn't go to the extremes of soul-searching is not as good, and is less what a novel should be? If you're willing to believe that, you might as well close this book and abandon your project. In reality, there are as many types of novels as people writing them.

Willa Cather's description is simple and personal:

> A novel, it seems to me, is merely a work of imagination in which a writer tries to present the experiences and emotions of a group by the light of his own. That is what he really does, whether his method is "objective" or "subjective."

From another angle, Scott Meredith said:

> A novel is a description of events stemming from a problem and eventually resulting in resolution of that problem. To put it another way, it is what happens when someone has a problem and overcomes it.

The idea of struggle and conflict as the key to the plot is echoed by anyone who takes novel writing seriously. Why is this necessary? Robert Penn Warren, Pulitzer Prize-winning novelist and critic, provides a psychological link:

To put it bluntly: No conflict, no story. If we do find a totally satisfactory adjustment in life, we tend to sink into the drowse of the accustomed. Only when our surroundings—or we ourselves—become problematic again do we wake up and feel that surge of energy which is life. And life more abundantly lived is what we seek.

Some kind of resolution of the problem is, owing to the very nature of fiction, promised. . . . We do not know how that story of our own life is going to come out. We do not know what it will mean.

Stories stir up our feelings. And people need to feel more. The novel offers an opportunity to sustain those feelings longer and with more lasting effect.

Honoré de Balzac brought the novel close to the autobiography when he said: "The most moving novels are autobiographical studies, or narratives of events submerged in the ocean of the world."

THE SHORT STORY

The short story requires particular skills in compact, or "tight," writing. There is a single significant, climactic episode in the central character's life. The moral or theme is integrated in the action. It opens with the crisis, or close to it. There is a climax, a struggle, and a conclusion. Usually, major change takes place in the main character, since there is no time to develop this, but he is left in a different place (often as the result of a decision he made), and feeling better. The tempo is a steady climb, unlike the novel with its many ups and downs and long stretches. These are in no way rules, since many experienced writers create change in character for better or worse.

In 1929, John Gallishaw proposed a diagram for the short story, and the plotted story has not changed much since then. In the diagram, the line A–D represents limitless time. B–C is the time portrayed in the story, also "the ordinary humdrum emotional level along which the life of the ordinary man or woman runs." From C, "the story must raise the reader to point 'E'— that place of heightened awareness and emotion the author wants him to experience."

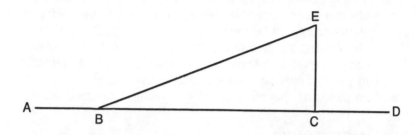

Styles have changed in short stories, so that the field is wide open for more abstract forms than in the past. There are no longer taboos. Any idea you have will fit some magazine, from fundamentalist religion to uninhibited sex. The story theme should be a strong one. Show characters in action. The short story is an emotional jolt, rather than the leisurely ebb and flow of the novel.

The short story can be more impressionistic because its characters need not be round. It contains one or two settings and goes light on transitions, but the joints should be tight fitting. Illusion, rather than reality, is germane to the short work. But the impression of life is at the heart of all fiction. Matisse, the great French Impressionist, showed a lady a painting of his—a nude woman—and she said, "But a woman isn't like that." Matisse answered, "It isn't a woman, madame, it's a picture."

The same sentiment was expressed by George Bernard Shaw when someone criticized *Pygmalion* for not representing real life. "That," said Shaw, "is the job of the Movietone News." So the short story can exercise another creative muscle in your representation of your life. It can project an impression or symbolic message that high points or peak experiences have for us all. This suggests that the short story is at its best when it deals with universal themes and experiences.

There's a rich field of forms in the short story other than the tightly plotted story. And it's one of the best ways to sharpen your writing skills. It may be simple, but it's not easy to write because every word must count.

The *short short* is even more difficult to write for the same reason. Within one or two pages, a highly intense moment of your life can be captured. It should have everything that goes into a short story, but be more condensed. In structure, there is a long beginning, a long middle, and one short scene for the end.

Other short works are character studies, a cameo memoir, a mood piece. These are more related to personal history and need no plot, but they should have a strong, universal theme.

DRAMATIC FORMS

The play, more than any other medium, arises from our primitive drives. Every child begins to play-act, to make-believe —as soon as he or she can walk and talk.

Theater is a collective experience. To be with others, to share an experience with hundreds of others, multiplies its impact. An audience contributes its magic, when a group reacts as one mammoth being, and interacts with the players. It's a social experience for the playgoer, and it's a collective *art*. The written play is only a blueprint for a final production involving cooperative efforts of actors, director, producer, designers, musicians, technicians, and staff. The whole is bigger than the sum of its parts, and the outcome depends on how well the artists involved put their characters in action. It is the only way the playwright has to tell the story—through dialogue (a form of action) and physical action.

The autobiographer selects from his life's events a rounded episode, a story within a story, but from this dramatized section, the audience knows the whole person. Because of the pressure of time, this form calls for a more impressionistic and compressed style in its presentation of life. A play can contain only a partial or thematic autobiography. Frequently a new playwright, bursting with elaborate feelings, will write as his first play the entire history of mankind from the dawn of civilization. The effort usually fails as disastrously as a person learning to cook who insists on a first menu of *pâté en croûte*, beef Stroganoff, asparagus with hollandaise sauce, and baked Alaska. (I taught cooking for years, and these are the actual favorite dishes chosen by beginning cooks.)

It's safer to choose the most outstanding crisis of your life and stress the struggle and the point it brought out. Chances are that the characters and the setting of this episode are already delineated by a real-life event. Then adjust the characters in a way that is "larger than life." But it is you who will be speaking through them all. If a villain is being villainous, it is you showing the manner of villainy and saying to the audience, "See how rotten he is, how he did that to me and why, and what happened to me and others as a result."

The real-life *persona* (C. G. Jung's term for the face we present to the world) is a mask—it is many masks, as we change hats and faces for the various roles we must play to survive in society. As a playwright we do the same. A play becomes an ideal method of showing off our different selves. Michael Chekhov said of this:

> In order to make (his different selves) wearable on the stage with sincerity, truth and artistic dignity, the playwright has to find and clothe his people (types) with the individual attributes that will transform them into the masks (characters) through which he will speak. He has to become the masks themselves for the duration of his creativity. For only these so-called masks can give him true opportunities to express himself anew each time and in each case and with utmost ingenuity and originality.

As for structure, the classic breakdown is three acts, while today's American theater seems to favor two—but the number of acts will depend on the nature of the play, the producer's financial limitation, and the local cultural traditions of the playgoer. Dramatists of other countries are devoted to three or even more acts because their audiences like to socialize and eat during intermissions.

Drama of sufficient length—at least one hour for a teleplay —can contain a subplot. The protagonist has a group of people on his side, the antagonist has his followers, so that there seem to be two small armies in combat. This is the main plot. The subplot is an important feature in drama. It involves a third grouping, not integrated into the main plot, not dependent on it and unaltered by the outcome of the main action.

The fundamental structure of fiction—beginning, middle,

and end—parallels acts I, II, and III. In Act I, all problems are presented. You'll often hear a writer agonizing over his "Act II curtain," meaning the climax, or most intense moment, or the Black Moment, when it appears all is lost and there's no way out. In Act III, suspense is maintained. Martin Esslin said that "expectations must be aroused, but never, until the last curtain, wholly fulfilled; the action must seem to be getting nearer to the objective yet never reach it entirely before the end."

The contemporary scene is totally permissive as to form. Esslin again:

> In a film by Antonioni or Altman, just as in a play by Beckett or Ionesco, we may well no longer ask the question which most controversial drama poses for the spectator: what's going to happen next? but the more general question: what's happening?

Whichever direction is your decision, there is only one rule: the audience must not be bored for a minute. It is captive, unlike the readers of the novel, which takes many hours to read, but which the reader can put down to get up and move around.

Varieties of form are endless. The one-act play corresponds to the short story. Only one situation is needed to bring the play to a climax. The main action starts late and not much character change takes place, as in some short stories. There are no wasted words, but a clear presentation with the problems at the beginning. The precision required makes this a difficult play to write. But if you have a short, intense episode to present, this is an ideal vehicle.

In the film media, the camera has an advantage comparable to the scope of the novel. It can serve as the author's intention to focus on particular visuals and details. Settings can be real, whereas in a play the scenery is painted and epic events such as the elements and earthquakes are suggested by dialogue, lighting, and off-stage sounds. The story has extra ways of moving along through close-ups, when a slight facial or body movement has an explicit meaning. But in the long run, it's the story and the way it's told that holds the interest of the audience. Illusion adds excitement in that the audience is allowed to fill in with its own imagination.

I've said that your choice of drama depends on certain technical and artistic demands. That's only half true. If the smell of the greasepaint is your nectar, you've been bitten by the theater bug. My sympathies. There is no known cure.

EXERCISE 1. SCENES

PURPOSE OF THIS EXERCISE

To begin to practice specific ways to achieve specific effects in the complete scene. The scene is like a miniature story. Keep in mind this is an exercise to develop skill, not a hard and fast rule for scene writing.

INSTRUCTIONS

Write a complete scene, chosen from one of the basic scene purposes on page 172. Include specific points and underline the sentence demonstrating these points:

a. *A meeting in the flesh.* No phone conversation. Main character speaks first (the one who gets the words in first gets the spotlight). Make sure whom the story is about. There should be a clash—with cause.

b. *Purpose.* State explicitly. Anybody can state it.

c. *Conclusive act.* Physical act. Not dialogue. Must fulfill at least one function: end the scene; demonstrate the disposal of purpose; actors depart.

d. *Scene plot step.* Summary of action in terms of disposal of purpose. It is a dramatized action step. Anyone can do it in the story, in any way. Use only when you need a specialized effect.

EXAMPLE (FROM A STUDENT'S CHILDHOOD):
Scene purpose chosen is "to get a consent" with an "abandonment" ending.

> With the typical wisdom of the typical four-year-old, Cathy knew just how far she could go

before her mother either gave in, or started screaming, or both.

MEETING: She stood fiddling with the door of the birdcage in the breakfast nook, and *watched her mother in the kitchen.*

"Why can't I take Rosie out? *Come on,* **PURPOSE:** *Mommy, lemme take him out."*

"Because Rosie's been out four times today. And you were rough. Birds shouldn't be pulled out by their feet. If they don't want to come out, they should be left alone. Anyway, it's time to wash your hands for dinner."

"But it's *my bird.* Uncle Morris said!"

"Uncle Morris doesn't live here and have to watch what you do to the poor thing."

"Only once more, Mommy. I'll be very, very gentle. Please, Mommy, please— Mommy—"

The sounds of dinner-making became banging noises. "Do what you want—I'm getting a headache from you!"

Cathy's chubby fist was already in the cage. Rosie backed into a corner, but Cathy reached in and grabbed him, holding one of his feet between her thumb and forefinger. With a burst of desperation, Rosie pecked at Cathy's finger like a woodpecker. The shocked little girl hesitated for a moment as she looked to see if her finger was still attached. She started to go to her mother, getting ready to **CONCLUSIVE** cry, but caught herself short. *Shutting the* **ACT:** *cage door with a bang,* she said, "Mommy, I changed up my mind."

"That's nice, honey. Get ready for dinner."

Holding her arm as if it were broken, **PLOT STEP:** *Cathy stared at the bird, wondering if it had teeth, and how to get its mouth open to find out.*

Try writing all twelve scene purposes with three different endings each—a total of thirty-six scenes. By that time, you will be quite facile at writing clear scene purposes. Go over each and make sure each scene does what it says it does.

EXERCISE 2. DRAMATIZING FACTS

PURPOSE OF THIS EXERCISE
All you do is recreate. Facts are dramatic.

INSTRUCTIONS
State a fact out of your life's experiences. Dramatize it. Make use of visual, sensual images, such as colors, tactile feeling.

EXAMPLE (FROM A STUDENT'S TRAVEL ADVENTURE):

The fact: We picked our way through the ruins.

Dramatized: We picked our way among the speckled stones and dust, the weeds struggling to survive, heaps of sand, the broken blocks and shapeless fragments, among patches of green bramble and spiky camel's thorn.

EXERCISE 3. DETAIL

PURPOSE OF THIS EXERCISE
To begin to think in terms of specific detail to assist in telling your story.

INSTRUCTIONS
Write a short scene or paragraph, using selected detail.

EXAMPLE (FROM A STUDENT'S SHORT STORY ABOUT A SEA VOYAGE):
One foot at a time, through the dining room, she made it to her table, the new and cheerful one near the porthole, and

thoughtfully, near the exit. It was her second try at dinner. Alfredo took aim and jabbed the menu into her hand as he swung back and forth, a pendulum. The gold letters on his jacket, "S.S. Italia," made her dizzy as they blurred past her. She gathered her reserve courage to face the elaborate menu and began to read the hand-lettered ornate items: *Asparagi alla Florentina* (Asparagus Florentine style); *Coniglio in Agrodolce* (Sweet and sour rabbit); *Ravioli; Anguilla alla Parmigiana* (Eels with parmesan cheese). . . .

EXERCISE 4. TEMPO

PURPOSE OF THIS EXERCISE
To get the feel of various tempos.

INSTRUCTIONS
Take one situation and write a paragraph using a slow tempo, then a fast tempo. Comment on which suits the meaning of the sequence best.

EXAMPLE (AN OLDER STUDENT, EXPLORING AN EXPERIENCE FROM THE OBJECTIVE POINT OF VIEW):

(Slow tempo, using slow-moving verbs, round vowels, longer sentences):

For a long time, the fragile, bent figure pondered over the corner of the envelope staring at her through the bottom of the door. She smoothed her dress and prepared to face the contents. "One way or another, I'll let you know, Mother. One way or another," he had told her.

(Staccato tempo—same material):

The little old lady stood by the door. She couldn't just pick it up. She hesitated a few moments, looking at the little white corner of the letter sticking through the door. She had to face it—she had to face it one way or another. It was his decision. Her only boy. She fiddled with her dress, gaining a few seconds before picking it up.

READINGS

CASSILL, R. V. *Writing Fiction.* Englewood Cliffs, N.J.: Prentice-Hall, 1975. A wonderful little book with all the basic principles you will need to get started. Examples from the works of some good writers.

CHEKHOV, MICHAEL. *To the Director and Playwright.* New York: Harper & Row, 1963. One of the best books about the art of theater by a famous teacher and brilliant actor, nephew of Anton Chekhov.

COWARD, NOEL. *Play Parade.* Garden City, N.Y.: Garden City Publishing Co., 1939. A collection of plays by the master of light comedy and sophisticated plays. Coward was one of the most versatile men of theater—he acted, directed, and wrote the music and lyrics for many of his own plays.

EGRI, LAJOS. *The Art of Dramatic Writing.* New York: Simon & Schuster, 1946. A marvelous book with everything you'll need to know about writing plays. Easy to learn from and extremely well written.

ELWOOD, MAREN. *Characters Make Your Story.* Boston: The Writer, 1945. *Write the Short Short.* Boston: The Writer, 1947. A fine teacher gives her beautifully worked-out system of planning for writing the time-honored plotted story, using thoroughly worked-out characters as a springboard.

ESSLIN, MARTIN. *An Anatomy of Drama.* New York: Hill & Wang, 1977. A recognized British scholar, critic, director, and producer wrote this treasure of a book containing the essence of the art of dramatic presentation.

FORSTER, E. M. *Aspects of the Novel.* New York: Harcourt Brace & Co., 1927. One of the most highly praised books about writing in general with special attention to the novel. Forster writes in a very spirited and amusing style, and is one of the great novelists in the English language.

GALLISHAW, JOHN. *Twenty Problems of the Fiction Writer.* New York: G. P. Putnam's Sons, 1929. An old basic text with all the fine points about writing the "old-fashioned" formal type of well-made story. Gallishaw emphasizes the short story, but the principles apply to all fiction.

JAMES, HENRY. *The Future of the Novel.* New York: Vintage Books, 1956. He has a surprisingly feminist viewpoint and wrote understandingly about women, in addition to being one of the most readable of the great American writers. He discusses mostly the art element in writing.

LUBBOCK, PERCY. *The Craft of Fiction.* New York: The Viking Press, 1976. An established standard for the serious student. A bit heavy to read, but contains much to learn about fiction.

MACGOWAN, KENNETH. *A Primer of Playwriting.* Garden City, N.Y.: Doubleday & Co., 1962. A small but tightly packed book with all the basics of a very professional approach to playwriting.

MAUGHAM, W. SOMERSET. *Points of View.* New York: Bantam Books, 1961. Magnificent studies and viewpoints on the subject of writing and writers.

TRAPNELL, COLES. *Teleplay, An Introduction to Television Writing.* New York: Hawthorn Books, 1974. An excellent book for the beginner. It explains, shows forms, and gives examples including an entire teleplay.

12

The Final Stages: Polishing and Publishing

> Don't *write about:*
> *racial intermarriage*
> *sexual perversion*
> *a child as a villain*
> *funerals*
> *surgical operations*
> *courtroom scenes*
> *explicit sex*
> *romance between older people.*
>
> —From a book on writing, 1952
>
> *There are very few taboos left in the book publishing business.*
>
> —From a book on writing, 1974

Maybe you didn't start out with the idea of selling, or maybe you need to protect your family's public image, or you just don't think your book will be good enough—but selling it is always a possibility. It's difficult, but not an impossible dream. Think of all the publishers who have to produce a certain number of profitable books to stay in business, the film houses, and television air time that have to be filled. They are all looking for material, something interesting and different. People don't often see their lives as being interesting to others, but I'm willing to bet that you have done something in your life that others could profit from economically, physically, intellectually, or spiritually.

187

Acquaint yourself with the current market trends by reading trade magazines on writing and books like *The Writer's Market,* an annual publication. Libraries carry them. Literary agents are swamped with submissions, but that doesn't mean yours won't get to them. A careful submission has a better chance than most material in their daily "sludge pile"—much of it thrown together without much thought and with misguided hopes of easy money and fame. A knowledge of the mechanics of submission is essential. Here are the broad categories.

LENGTHS AND LAYOUTS: PREPARING THE MANUSCRIPT

It's only possible to give you a general idea of lengths and layouts. This will vary with publishers, production companies, and television networks.

For books and short stories, figure approximately 250 words per page, typed—double-spaced.

For film scripts, figure approximately 1¾ minutes playing time per page. For television scripts, figure sixty pages for forty-five minutes playing time (without commercial breaks).

Novels	120–330 pages (30,000–50,000 words)
	May be as long as 240–1,500 pages (60,000–250,000 words)
Short stories	8–20 pages (2,000–5,000 words)
Short short stories	2–12 pages (500–1,800 words)
Stage plays	100–150 pages
Screen plays	130–160 pages
TV plays (playing time)	
½ hour	40 pages
1 hour	80 pages
90 minutes	120 pages

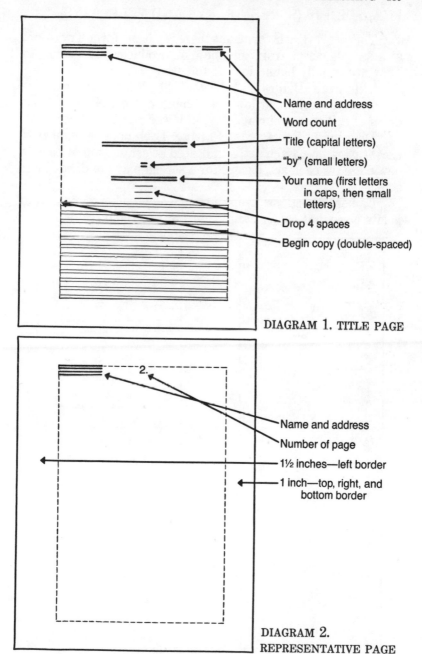

DIAGRAM 1. TITLE PAGE

DIAGRAM 2.
REPRESENTATIVE PAGE

FILM SCRIPTS (SCREEN PLAYS AND TELEPLAYS)

These will vary in form, but there is a basic form. Try to look at a sample script from the show or producer you submit to. They are usually bound in soft folders.

Title page (Diagram 3): "Title," "by," and your name as indicated. Copyright in lower left-hand corner. Name and address of agent, or your address, in lower right-hand corner.

Diagram 5: Representative page. Each page is numbered, except page one. Each act is indicated at center, top of page, a new page for each act, except for a screen play not divided into acts.

Camera directions: keep as simple as possible to make your points clear, but camera angles are left to the director.

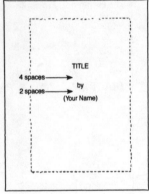

DIAGRAM 3.

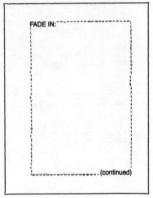

DIAGRAM 4.

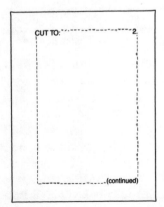

DIAGRAM 5.

SAMPLE SCENE

FADE IN:

INT. – MONA'S KITCHEN – MONA

as she fixes a milkshake in the blender, her drawn face becomes alert as if she hears something.

> MONA
> Doreen.
> (short pause)
> Doreen! Is that you?

A DOOR SLAMS, MONA drops what she is doing, quickly wipes her hands, and starts to leave.

DOREEN enters. Her clothes are disheveled, and there is a prominent bruise under her left eye.

CLOSE – MONA

> MONA
> (tries to keep calm)
> Honey! What happened?

THE MANUSCRIPT

Use a new ribbon for each manuscript—good, dark, and clear nylon or cotton or the new carbon-type ribbons.

Use a good letter-sized bond, sixteen- or twenty-pound weight. Or use a correction-type paper. Or a self-correcting typewriter.

Word count: for short works, count every word. For longer works, *estimate* word count by taking four average pages, counting the words, and taking the average. (Hyphenated and contracted words count as one.)

Always double-space everything, including footnotes and bibliographies. Correct errors as you go. If there are too many, retype the page. Authors, intent on saving costs of paper and typing, don't realize that double-spacing makes the manuscript more readable to those considering buying it. Also, single-spacing costs more to have copy-edited, proofread, and typeset, and adversely affects the pricing of the book.

If manuscript is a few pages long, fold it in thirds and send it in a document-sized envelope. Or fold double in a manila envelope. If eight pages or more, mail it flat between corregated carton paper ½-inch larger all around. *Do not* staple or clip pages together—leave them loose and put rubber bands around carton paper.

Manuscripts should be mailed first class, except book manuscripts, which go (pages loose) in a corrugated box and are sent express. *Never roll* a manuscript. Always enclose a stamped, self-addressed envelope, folded neatly.

Don't enclose a letter unless you have something special to say.

Anything you write is automatically protected by the new copyright law (of January 1, 1978) for life—plus 50 years. You can register this copyright for $10.00 if you want more protection against possible legal problems. For a brief summary of this subject, consult guides such as current editions of the *Writer's Market* or the *World Almanac,* or special books about literary laws. For a free information kit, send to the Copyright Office, Library of Congress, Washington, D.C. 20559, and specify the category of your work.

Never, never send out a manuscript without keeping a clean, current copy in your files.

REVISING AND POLISHING

Revising is not the same as polishing, but they go hand in hand. Revising is rethinking and reworking a story or part of it so that it carries the weight, impact, and impression you envisioned.

Don't regard revising as something mechanical. It's a creative part of writing. It may mean putting the beginning at the end and the end in the middle, or conjuring up a stronger ending. It may mean condensing two characters into one or throwing one out. A character may work better as upper class or lower class. A story may have more punch in another setting, for example, changing a suburban home to an isolated mountain cabin.

Polishing is what you do when your script is finished. You correct typos (typing errors) and spelling errors. Armed with a thesaurus or dictionary of synonyms, you take time to hunt for better or more sparkling words, words that say what you want to say—better. You condense paragraphs, cut superfluous words, arrange sentences for greater clarity and unity, and tend to your grammar.

But first, put the manuscript away for a few days or weeks —however long it takes to come back to it with a fresh eye. Then read it end to end before tackling the final job. But don't become obsessed with this. Find the right balance between too little and too much polishing. The following checklist will help guide you —and serve as an instant refresher course of the pertinent points in this book.

Ask yourself the following questions:

STORY CHECKLIST

OVERVIEW:

1. Does the story accomplish what I set out to do?

2. Does it have the magic of transmuting my life to fiction and letting the reader know what kind of person I am?

3. Is my presence felt the way I want it to be?

4. Would I read this and enjoy it if I had not written it?

5. What kind of person or group would this story appeal to?

6. Does it have the emotional effect on the reader I wanted? What is it, specifically? (In one word.)

7. Do I feel a definite style of my own in the writing and the mood? Is it too weak? Can I bring it out more? Is it too strong and does it overpower the story?

8. What is my story? (In one sentence.)

9. What is the underlying theme?

THE STORY:

10. Is the story integrated with the theme, or am I preaching too much?

11. Is the story purpose clear enough for anyone to understand?

12. Are both forces that are in combat strong enough to make the story powerful, or interesting enough?

13. Does the story fill its form in terms of time span, substance of material?

14. Is it too thin for a novel?

15. Is there too much material for the length I gave it—should I *increase* the word length?

16. Is the story I selected really short-story length?

17. Would the idea come across better as a drama?

18. Something of importance must motivate the outcome. What is it?

19. Do I, the protagonist, achieve my goal dramatically? (Whether fiction or nonfiction.)

20. Will other people really care about the problem I've presented?

21. Does it sound as if I know what I'm talking about when I am dealing with issues, technical matter, data?

22. Am I sure I've done my best and feel it's ready to send out?

THE WRITING:

23. Are there enough sensory details? Visual effects?

24. Are my descriptions colorful? Do they convey the essence of the setting or person?

25. Did I use an interesting and broad enough vocabulary? Have I repeated a word or expression too often?

26. Does the dialogue sound natural? (Have I used a tape recorder to *speak* the lines, then transcribed them?)

27. Does the central character sound like me? Did I want him or her to sound like me as I am, or I'd like to sound?

28. Is there enough action? Have I shown it, not just told it?

29. Are there any cliches, trite expressions, or dull expressions I should upgrade?

30. Are there any sentences, speeches, or narration that are too long?

31. Have I summarized the story periodically?

32. Does it have that "What next?" pull?

THE CHARACTERS:

33. Does each character have a suitable name?

34. Is each name different from the others?

35. Is each character individualized so that he or she does not resemble another in personality or physically—unless it has a story purpose?

36. Is each character developed fully enough?

37. Does each character give the illusion of reality, of a living being?

38. Is each character necessary to the story?

39. Does each character use dialogue individual to that personality, so there is a variety of speech?

40. Have I clarified the motive of each character?

41. Have I given adequate descriptions of each character? Physically, psychologically?

STRUCTURE, CLARITY, UNITY, STYLE:

42. Have I injected frequent, brief story summaries or plot steps to remind readers of items they may have missed at some point? (Readers skip a lot.)

43. Have I checked the use of points of view, so that it's clear at all times who is speaking?

44. Have I made clear at all times where the action is taking place, and what it looks like?

45. Have I gone off on tangents that may disorient, bore, or otherwise lose the reader?

46. Have I sandwiched in dull information, in small bites?

47. Are there sections that are too talky? Can I put them into action?

48. Have I used any awkward expressions or sentence construction?

49. Have I waited too long to introduce the main characters and the problem?

50. Have I made it clear what kind of story it is at the beginning?

51. In the body of my story, does the interest and intensity rise as I wanted it to?

52. Does the action stop for too long a time in any spot?

53. Do I have enough complications? Are they valid? Are they interesting?

54. Do I have too many complications?

55. Have I pulled any surprises on the reader that are not fair, such as bringing in a new character too late to be well integrated into the story?

56. Have I dragged out the ending?

57. Is my climax too weak?

58. Is my ending anticlimactic?

59. Have I been courageous in cutting out extraneous matter?

60. Have I left any odds and ends dangling at the end?

61. Am I being objective about revising and polishing so that personal hangups don't interfere with doing what is best for the story?

62. Did I get enough rich material out of my life? Personal history data? Detail? Anecdotes?

MARKETING AND THE PUBLISHING SCENE

We are concerned only with publishing *your* story in some form, so this will not resemble the usual manual on how to become a writer. Books on writing talk about how to find ideas, how to "slant" material—find out what a publisher publishes, then tailor a story to his style and needs. You'll discover the thousands of markets, national and international, and the hundreds of specialized and commercial stories and articles.

Of course, if you've become excited about writing and decide to pursue it as a profession, by all means get involved with workshops and conferences. Subscribe to writers' magazines, and read as many classics and current books on writing, some of which are specialized in fields of writing. Haunt bookstores and browse among the books most closely resembling your own in subject matter. Look for the way the book is put together in terms of layout, jacket design, copy and quotes on the back cover. Make notes on the publishing houses and which ones produce the kind of work you like best.

Study the book review sections in the newspaper, and get the feeling of how different publishers *publicize* their books. Does it feel dignified, tacky, too commercial? Which approach appeals to you most and which fits your book the best?

Consult *Literary Market Place* (LMP), a Bowker publication, which is updated annually. The Bible for the publishing industry, it contains a listing of key personnel at almost all publishing houses, as well as listings of agents, advertising agencies, a classification of publishing houses by subject matter, and other valuable information. Look for it in your local library.

For short stories and articles you will need to study magazines. Browse through them and study the type of stories the magazine publishes, length, style, choice of subjects, and take note of the lead article. Also study the advertisers—this tells you what kind of reader the magazine is aimed at.

Consult the *Writer's Market.* Each publication will give its guidelines for submissions. It also lists agents, literary services, writer's clubs, annual conferences, organizations, and any other basic information you'll need to get started.

Some magazines will send you a free sample copy on request—look for the offer in the specific magazine's listing. Some magazines ask a fee for a sample copy. To send for a free sample, drop them a postcard with a request such as:

Dear Sir or Madame or Ms.:

So that I may study your magazine in order to slant material to your requirements, I would be most appreciative if you would send me a sample copy of your publication.

Sincerely,

Watch for book fairs in your local calendar of events or consult your bookseller. Other events such as authors autographing books in department stores, writing conferences, and booksellers conventions can be interesting for the feeling of what it's like to promote a book. Talk to the authors if you can, and anyone from the publishing houses—just gather information about how you feel they treat their authors, and how hard they work to sell the book. It's a way you can talk to professionals informally and pick up the flavor and facts of the trade. You may even decide you hate the book business.

For magazine pieces, an agent isn't necessary but editors prefer a query letter. You can assume your material will be read. Don't do sneaky things like inserting a hair off your head, or a page upside down to know if the material was read. Readers and editors are on to all the tricks, and it won't help you.

For large works such as books and stage or screen plays, and any television product, an agent is a must. This can be difficult. But there again, it will partially depend on your material. Partially, because there are historical cases of best-sellers that were rejected on numerous submissions before someone recognized their value.

Use a "query" letter before you send a short or long piece to an editor or an agent. This saves everyone time. They may have done a book or article on this very subject recently. (You should have checked this out—see what they've published in the last year.) For example:

Dear (actual name when possible):

I have written a short story, 3,500 words in length. The main character is a young man who baby-sits to work his way through medical school.

His employment agency sends him to a single mother who happens to be the assistant to the chief of staff in obstetrics at the school hospital. She is using an advanced method of child rearing and is skeptical that this gentle young man will be able to handle her two precocious children.

The crucial scene is a touch-and-go contest with the challenging children. They all win.

May I send the story for your consideration?

Sincerely,

The best advice anyone can give you is to *persist* in both upgrading your material and submitting, getting professional help from teachers and others who understand the business end.

Avoid companies that offer to help you publish your own book unless you know an author who has used one. Many famous works started that way, but in your case—telling your story—I don't recommend it. It's usually very expensive and full of promises that may be suspect. At least check out your book with a teacher or other professional before taking this risk.

Publishing for profit may not be your goal. *Sharing* your book with family or friends is a frequent goal. To share your story, use a printer—interview several and get their reactions. Take estimates, but first know exactly what you want. Let them see a draft of the manuscript with a listing of the number of diagrams, photographs, or any special artwork. Hiring graphic artists can run into enormous expense.

Two women in autobiography workshops had especially interesting experiences. One did a simple, charming story of her grandmother, in interview form. She taped it, and wrote the grandmother's words as they sounded. She had the book printed, with sepia photos included. This was done only as a holiday gift for all the members of the family. But as she showed the book in workshops as an example, half the people wanted to buy it! The other student wrote a short family history. As she showed her book around, several people asked her to write their family histories. She is doing so, having learned the system and resources, and has developed a lucrative profession.

Money and fame are popular goals, but nothing beats a system that helps one face the future purified, clarified, and focused. The potential benefits of writing the story of your life are unlimited. And from this moment on, you will begin to create new stories.

READINGS

CARROLL, GORDON, ed. *Writing, Revising, and Editing.* Garden City, N.Y.: Doubleday & Co., 1969. A combined work of teachers and editors from the Famous Writers School.

ELWOOD, MAREN. *111 Don'ts for Writers.* Boston: The Writer, 1949. A beautifully organized and practical checklist for writers to help them remember all the important points about each phase of their work.

KOESTER, JANE, and HILLMANN, BRUCE JOEL, eds. *The Writer's Market.* Cincinnati: Writer's Digest, 1978. An annual publication. The basic reference and complete guide to markets and marketing.

MATHIEU, ARON, ed. *The Creative Writer.* Cleveland: Writer's Digest, 1968. Articles on some major aspects of commercial writing.

MEREDITH, SCOTT. *Writing to Sell.* New York: Harper & Row, 1977. A breezy, informative, and practical guide to the subject of its title by a leading literary agent.

Bibliography

ADAMS, HENRY. *The Education of Henry Adams.* New York: Random House, 1931.

ALBERTI, ROBERT E., Ph.D., and EMMONS, MICHAEL L., Ph.D. *Your Perfect Right.* San Luis Obispo, Calif.: Impact, Box 1094, 93406, 1974.

ALCOTT, LOUISA MAY. *Her Life, Letters, and Journals.* Edited by Edna D. Cheney. Boston: Little, Brown & Co., 1919.

ANDERSON, SHERWOOD. *A Story Teller's Story.* New York: Huebsch, 1924.

AUGUSTINE, SAINT. *Confessions.* Translated by Julie Kernan. New York: Doubleday & Co., 1962.

BAKER, M. E. PENNY. *Meditation: A Step Beyond with Edgar Cayce.* New York: Pinnacle Books, 1973.

BALDWIN, CHRISTINA. *One to One.* New York: M. Evans & Co., 1977.

BASHKIRTSEFF, MARIE. *The Journal of a Young Artist.* Translated by Mary J. Serrano. New York: E. P. Dutton, 1923.

BATES, E. STUART. *Inside Out: An Introduction to Autobiography.* New York: Sheridan House, 1937.

BENSON, HERBERT, M.D. *The Relaxation Response.* New York: Avon Books, 1975.

BERGER, JOSEF, and BERGER, DOROTHY. *Small Voices.* New York: Paul S. Eriksson, 1966.

BERNE, ERIC, M.D. *Games People Play.* New York: Grove Press, 1967.

BOMBECK, ERMA. *At Wit's End.* New York: Fawcett Crest Books, 1975. Also *I Lost Everything in the Post-Natal Depression.* New York: Fawcett Crest Books, 1978, and many others too numerous to list.

BRADLEY, MIKE; DANCHIK, LONNIE; FAGER, MARTY; and WODETSKI, TOM. *Unbecoming Men.* New York: Times Change Press, 1971.

BRANDE, DOROTHEA. *Becoming a Writer.* New York: Harcourt, Brace & Co., 1934.

BUCK, PEARL S. *My Several Worlds.* New York: The John Day Co., 1954.

BURR, ANNA ROBESON. *The Autobiography: A Critical and Comparative Study.* Cambridge, Mass.: Houghton Mifflin Co., 1909.

CAINE, LYNN. *Widow.* New York: William Sloane Associates, 1964.

CARROLL, GORDON, ed. *Writing, Revising, and Editing.* Garden City, N.Y.: Doubleday & Co., 1969.

CASANOVA, JACQUES. *The Memoirs of Jacques Casanova.* New York: Macmillan, 1962.

CASE, PATRICIA ANN. *How to Write Your Autobiography, or Preserving Your Family Heritage.* Santa Barbara, Calif.: Woodbridge Press Publishing Co., 1977.

CASSILL, R. V. *Writing Fiction.* Englewood Cliffs, N.J.: Prentice-Hall, 1975.

CATHER, WILLA. *On Writing.* New York: Alfred A. Knopf, 1949.

CELLINI, BENVENUTO. *The Autobiography of Benvenuto Cellini.* Garden City, N.Y.: Doubleday & Co., 1946.

CHASE, STUART. *The Tyranny of Words.* New York: Harcourt, Brace & Co., 1938.

CHEKHOV, MICHAEL. *To the Director and Playwright.* New York: Harper & Row, 1963.

CHUTE, MARCETTE. *The Search for God.* New York: E. P. Dutton, 1958.

COOLEY, THOMAS. *Educated Lives: The Rise Of Modern Autobiography in America.* Columbus, Ohio: Ohio State University Press, 1976.

Contact Quarterly. P.O. Box 297, Stinson Beach, CA 94970.

COWARD, NOEL. *Play Parade.* Garden City, N.Y.: Garden City Publishing Co., 1939.

COWLEY, MALCOLM, ed. *Writers at Work.* New York: The Viking Press, 1958.

DEAN, JOHN W., III. *Blind Ambition: The White House Years.* New York: Simon & Schuster, 1976.

DE QUINCEY, THOMAS. *Confessions of an English Opium Eater.* Jacksonville, FL: Heritage House, 1950.

Developmental Psychology Today. Del Mar, Calif.: CRM Books, 1971.

DIXON, J. T., and FLACK, D. D. *Preserving Your Past.* Garden City, N.Y.: Doubleday & Co., 1977.

DONAHUE, PHIL. *Donahue, My Own Story.* New York: Simon & Schuster, 1979.

DRAZNIN, YAFFA. *The Family Historian's Handbook.* New York: Harcourt Brace Jovanovich, 1978.

DUNCAN, ISADORA. *My Life.* New York: Boni and Liveright, 1972.

EGRI, LAJOS. *The Art of Dramatic Writing.* New York: Simon & Schuster, 1946.

EHRLICH, IDA. *Instant Vocabulary.* New York: Pocket Books, 1969.

ELWOOD, MAREN. *Characters Make Your Story.* Boston: The Writer, 1945.

————. *Write the Short Short.* Boston: The Writer, 1947.

————. *111 Don'ts for Writers.* Boston: The Writer, 1949.

ERIKSON, ERIK H. *Childhood and Society.* New York: W. W. Norton & Co., 1963.

————. *Identity, Youth and Crisis.* New York: W. W. Norton & Co., 1968.

ESSLIN, MARTIN. *An Anatomy of Drama.* New York: Hill & Wang, 1977.

EVANS, RICHARD I. *B. F. Skinner, The Man and His Ideas.* New York: E. P. Dutton, 1968.

FARADAY, ANN. *The Dream Game.* New York: Harper & Row, 1976.

FINK, DAVID HAROLD, M.D. *Release from Nervous Tension.* New York: Simon & Schuster, 1962.

FLESCH, RUDOLF. *The Art of Plain Talk.* New York: Harper & Bros., 1946.

————. *The Art of Readable Writing.* New York: Collier Books, 1978.

FORBES, ESTHER. *Paul Revere and the World He Lived in.* Boston: Houghton Mifflin Co., 1942.

FORD, BETTY. *The Times of My Life.* New York: Harper & Row, 1978

FORSTER, E. M. *Aspects of the Novel.* New York: Harcourt, Brace & Co., 1927.

FRANK, ANNE. *The Diary of a Young Girl.* Garden City, N.Y.: Doubleday & Co., 1952.

FRANKEL, VIKTORE. *Man's Search for Meaning.* New York: Simon & Schuster, 1971.

FRANKLIN, BENJAMIN. *The Autobiography of Benjamin Franklin.* New York: A.S. Barnes & Co., 1944.

FREUD, SIGMUND. *The Basic Writings of Sigmund Freud.* Translated and edited with an Introduction by A. A. Brill. New York: Random House, 1938.

FUNK, WILFRED, and LEWIS, NORMAN. *30 Days to a More Powerful Vocabulary.* New York: Pocket Books, 1945.

GALLISHAW, JOHN. *Twenty Problems of the Fiction Writer.* New York: G. P. Putnam's Sons, 1929.

GANDHI, MOHANDAS K. *An Autobiography.* Boston: Beacon Press, 1957.

GARIS, ROBERT, ed. *Writing About Oneself.* Boston: D. C. Heath and Co., 1965.

GIBBON, EDWARD. *Memoirs of My Life.* New York: Funk & Wagnall's Co., 1969.

GOERTZEL, V., and GOERTZEL, M. G. *Cradles of Eminence.* Boston: Little, Brown & Co., 1962.

GOODMAN, ELLEN. *Turning Points.* New York: Doubleday & Co., 1979.

GRAY, BETTYANNE. *Manya's Story.* New York: Doubleday & Co., 1978.

GUITRY, SACHA. *If Memory Serves.* Garden City, N.Y.: Doubleday, Doran, 1935.

HALEY, ALEX. *Roots.* Garden City, N.Y.: Doubleday & Co., 1976.

HARRIS, THOMAS, M.D. *I'm O.K.—You're O.K.* New York: Harper & Row, 1969.

HELLMAN, LILLIAN. *An Unfinished Woman.* Boston: Little, Brown & Co., 1969.

HERRIGEL, EUGENE. *Zen in the Art of Archery.* New York: Pantneon Books, 1953.

HERRIOT, JAMES. *All Things Bright and Beautiful.* New York: Bantam Books, 1973.

HOLMES, JOHN HAYNES. *My Gandhi.* New York: Harper & Bros., 1953.

HOLT, JOHN. *Never Too Late.* New York: Delacorte Press, 1978.

ISHERWOOD, CHRISTOPHER. *Kathleen and Frank.* New York: Simon & Schuster, 1971.

JAMES, HENRY. *The Future of the Novel.* New York: Vintage Books, 1956.

JONG, ERICA. *Fear of Flying.* New York: Holt, Rinehart & Winston, 1973.

JOURARD, SIDNEY M. *The Transparent Self.* Princeton, N.J.: D. Van Nostrand Co., 1964.

JUNG, CARL GUSTAV. *Man and His Symbols.* Garden City, N.Y.: Doubleday & Co., 1964.

KAPLAN, LOUIS. *A Bible of American Autobiographies.* Madison, Wis.: University of Wisconsin Press, 1961.

KEEN, SAM, and FOX, ANNE VALLEY. *Telling Your Story: A Guide to Who You Are and Who You Can Be.* New York: Doubleday & Co., 1973.

LAGERLÖF, SELMA. *The Diary of Selma Lagerlöf.* Translated by Velma Swanston Howard. Garden City, N.Y.: Doubleday Doran, 1936.

LESSING, DORIS. *Particularly Cats.* New York: Simon & Schuster, 1978.

LUBBOCK, PERCY *The Craft of Fiction.* New York: The Viking Press, 1976.

MACGOWAN, KENNETH. *A Primer of Playwriting.* Garden City, N.Y.: Doubleday & Co., 1962.

MANSFIELD, KATHERINE. *The Journal of Katherine Mansfield.* Edited by John Middleton Murray. New York: Alfred A. Knopf, 1927.

MASLOW, ABRAHAM. *Toward a Psychology of Being.* Princeton, N.J.: D. Van Nostrand Co., 1968.

MATHIEU, ARON, ed. *The Creative Writer.* Cleveland, Ohio: Writer's Digest, 1968.

MAUGHAM, W. SOMERSET. *The Summing Up.* Garden City, N.Y.: Doubleday & Co., 1953.

————. *The Vagrant Mood.* Garden City, N.Y.: Doubleday & Co., 1953.

————. *A Writer's Notebook.* Garden City, N.Y.: Doubleday & Co., 1953.

MCCARTHY, MARY. *Memories of a Catholic Girlhood.* New York: Harcourt Brace & World, 1952.

MEREDITH, SCOTT. *Writing to Sell.* New York: Harper & Row, 1977.

MILLER, MERLE, and EVAN, RHODES. *Only You, Dick Daring.* New York: William Sloane Associates, 1964.

MISCH, GEORGE. *A History of Autobiography in Antiquity.* Cambridge, Mass.: Harvard University Press, 1951.

MOFFAT, MARY JANE, and PAINTER, CHARLOTTE, eds. *Revelations: Diaries of Women.* New York: Random House, 1975.

MUIR, EDWIN. *An Autobiography.* London: The Hogarth Press, 1954.

MUNTHE, AXEL. *The Story of San Michele.* London: The Albatross, 1948.

NIN, ANAÏS. *The Diary of Anaïs Nin.* 6 vols. Chicago: The Swallow Press, 1966.

PASCAL, ROY. *Design and Truth in Autobiography.* London: Routledge & Kegan Paul, 1960.

PORTER, ROGER J., and WOLF, H. R. *The Voice Within.* New York: Alfred A. Knopf, 1973.

PROGOFF, IRA. *At a Journal Workshop.* New York: Dialogue House Library, 1975.

REYNOLDS, PAUL R. *The Writing and Selling of Non-Fiction.* New York: Doubleday & Co., 1963.

ROBERTS, KENNETH. *I Wanted to Write.* New York: Doubleday & Co., 1949.

ROOSEVELT, ELEANOR. *This I Remember.* New York: Harper & Bros., 1949.

————. *The Autobiography of Eleanor Roosevelt.* New York: Harper & Row, 1961.

————. *On My Own.* New York: Harper & Bros., 1953.

ROUSSEAU, JEAN-JACQUES. *Confessions.* Baltimore: Penguin Books, 1954.

SAND, GEORGE. *The Intimate Journal of George Sand.* New York: John Day Co., 1929.

SECHRIST, ELSIE. *Dreams, Your Magic Mirror.* New York: Warner Books, 1974.

SHATTOCK, E. H. *An Experiment in Mindfulness.* New York: E. P. Dutton, 1960.

SHEEHY, GAIL. *Passages: Predictable Crises of Adult Life.* New York: E. P. Dutton, 1974.

SIMONS, GEORGE F. *Keeping Your Personal Journal.* New York: Paulist Press, 1978.

STANDEN, NIKA. *Reminiscence and Ravioli.* New York: William Morrow & Co., 1946.

STEINBECK, JOHN. *Travels with Charley.* New York: The Viking Press, 1963.

STRUNK, WILLIAM, JR., and WHITE, E. B. *The Elements of Style.* New York: The Macmillan Co., 1959.

THOREAU, HENRY DAVID. *Walden and Other Writings.* New York: Random House, 1950.

TOLSTOY, SOPHIE A. *The Diary of Tolstoy's Wife.* Translated by Alexander Werth. London: Victor Gollancz, 1928.

TRIMBLE, JOHN R. *Writing with Style.* Englewood Cliffs, N.J.: Prentice-Hall, 1975.

TOURNIER, PAUL. *A Place for You.* New York: Harper & Row, 1968.

WETHERED, H. N. *The Curious Art of Autobiography.* New York: Philosophical Library, 1956.

WOOLF, VIRGINIA. *A Writer's Diary.* New York: Harcourt, Brace, 1954.

The Writer's Market. Cincinnati, Ohio: A Writer's Digest Book, annual publication.

ZIEGLER, ISABELLE. *The Creative Writer's Handbook.* New York: Barnes & Noble, 1975.

INDEX